KT-446-306

your

TRAINING SKILLS

develop your
TRAINING SKILLS

Leslie Rae

KOGAN
PAGE

First published in 2001

Kogan Page Limited
120 Pentonville Road
London
N1 9JN
UK

Stylus Publishing Inc.
22883 Quicksilver Drive
Sterling
VA 20166-2012
USA

British Library Cataloguing in Publication Data

A CIP record for this book is available from the British Library.

ISBN 0 7494 3591 7

Typeset by JS Typesetting, Wellingborough, Northants
Printed and bound in Great Britain by Biddles Ltd, Guildford and King's Lynn

Contents

Preface   *vii*

1. **Getting Started and Moving On**   **1**
    Introduction; Progress; Induction; Progressive entry to practical
    training; The trainer as a learner; The Learning Log

2. **What Is a Trainer?**   **13**
    The role of the trainer: Training functions; The knowledge and skills
    of the effective trainer; Who is a trainer?; The 'Townsend' model of
    trainer types; Other trainer typology

3. **The Input Session**   **32**
    The basic approach; The planning and preparation of an input session;
    Presentation skills; Techniques for making the input session as
    effective as possible; Before the start of the input session; The training
    environment; What to do immediately prior to the event; A presenter's
    toolkit

4. **How Do I Get Them to Listen?**   **48**
    Opening a presentation or session; During the presentation or session;
    Some final thoughts on making your points

5. **Using Training Aids**   **64**
    A particular object; The presenter; The flipchart; The whiteboard;
    The overhead projector

6. **Other Training Aids**   81
    Handouts; Using handouts; Guidelines for writing handouts; Audio
    equipment; Videos; The computer – computer-assisted training/
    learning (CAT/CAL)

7. **More Than Just Talking**   95
    Buzz groups; Syndicates; Discussions; Demonstrations; Question
    and answer; Short group activities; Activity uses; Introductory
    activity; Icebreakers; Energizers or session shakers

8. **More Training Activity Approaches**   109
    Learning activity; Role playing; Case studies; Simulations; The
    in-tray or in-basket activity; Action mazes; Brainstorming; Computers
    (CBT); Action learning; Selecting the appropriate training strategy

9. **In-company Training**   130
    On-the-job training and self-training approaches; GAFO; Coaching;
    Mentoring; One-to-one instruction; Team development; Open
    learning; Computer-based training

10. **People in Training**   153
    Communication; Barriers to communication; Maslow's hierarchy
    of needs; The Johari Window; Neuro-linguistic Programming (NLP);
    The competence ladder

11. **Coping with People**   166
    Handling difficult replies to your questions; What are difficult
    people? First steps in handling situations; Conclusion

References and Recommended Reading   *179*

Index   *182*

Preface

You will read at the start of Chapter 1 that I describe training and the role of the trainer as one of the oldest, if not the oldest profession practised by the human race. Thus, on this rather naive concept, there have always been trainers, and there will always be trainers. An integral part of the human being, and to a more restrictive extent of animals, is the need to learn over a very extensive range of knowledge, skills and attitudes. The role of the trainer has changed considerably over the years, not least in the last 30 or 40, and there are significant signs that the next decade will see further, perhaps more revolutionary changes.

Entry to the role of trainer can be a frightening prospect indeed, and the purpose of this book is to try to describe what lies ahead for the prospective or new trainer, in terms of the three basic aspects of knowledge, skills and attitudes. The extent of what has to be developed as described in the book may, at first, appear to be as frightening as the prospect of becoming a trainer. But bear in mind that, although there is a lot to learn, there will be only restricted aspects to consider at first – which aspects depend on the specific roles required by the organization to which the trainer belongs. You will not be expected, in fact you would find it impossible, to be able to learn and do everything immediately. The skills of the effective trainer take time to develop and certainly require substantial support from training managers and other trainers.

Three words are in common use in the profession and these may need some definition. The descriptions are taken from *A Glossary of UK Training & Occupational Learning Terms* (2000) by the Institute of Training and Occupational Learning (ITOL), the glossary being produced by a working party of trainers, training managers and consultants from ITOL:

- **Training:** Any planned activity designed and performed to help an individual or a group to learn to perform a job or task effectively. (This activity can be an off-the-job or an on-the-job training course or workshop, an open learning package or an Internet/intranet program.)

- **Development:** A gradual personal growth or evolution of knowledge, skill, attitudes, behaviour that is gained through learning from a variety of experiences. (Usually applied to people with some existing skills, knowledge or attitudes wanting to improve, change employment or career paths or move to higher employment levels.)
- **Learning:** (1) A relatively permanent change in behaviour. (2) The acquisition or development of knowledge and understanding, skills and abilities, emotional competence and attitudes. Learning is both a process and an outcome and can be induced by training or self-learning/development.

The format of this book has been planned to cover all these areas and concentrates on the knowledge about the role that new, or relatively new trainers and their mentors or managers need to learn so that the problems of change can be made easier. But even so, as expressed above, movement to effectiveness takes time and is best described as a progressive development or increase in skills.

If you take from and give as much to the training role as I have tried to do as a trainer, training manager and consultant, there can be no doubt that you will also enjoy the experience tremendously.

I must express my thanks to all the learners, trainers, training managers and consultants with whom I have been associated over the years and who taught me so much about my trade. The trainer, every time he or she starts a training event of whatever nature, can be assured that they will finish the event having learnt something from both the event and the learners.

My thanks also to Philip Mudd and his colleagues at Kogan Page who have encouraged me to write about the subject of training and development (and write well!) for some years now.

Leslie Rae

Want to release your potential? Help others release theirs. ~ Pat Lynch

1
Getting Started and Moving On

Introduction

So you want to be a trainer? Or perhaps you are on the point of becoming one, or you have recently started to become one. Whichever the case may be you are on the threshold of one of the most challenging, interesting and satisfying professions, a profession that is currently in a state of development, the eventual stage of which is as yet unclear. But whatever the end stage one thing *is* clear: there will always be a need for skilled trainers, whatever their actual roles.

I would place the start of 'training' in an age before even the often-quoted 'oldest profession', as stone age man was the first trainer. He taught the youngsters to hunt mammoths, make stone tools, and eventually farm. Every increase in skill and knowledge followed from this original form of training to the present day – but how it has changed!

Training that once had an almost singular approach is now full of bewildering choices of approach, technique, methods and tools. If you are on this potentially frightening threshold, this book is for you, a book that sets out to offer you guidance and help through the first difficult months of professional entry.

You will not learn to become a trainer in an instant – to become this you will need to read books, attend a 'train the trainer' programme, watch training videos, perhaps follow Internet and intranet programs, and attend further development programmes. But above all you will need to gain as much hands-on, practical experience as you can by helping experienced trainers in their programme planning and preparation, and by assisting them in progressive stages with an actual course. This book should prepare you for these events, giving you information about how training and development is approached and helping you to become accustomed to the special language, the jargon, of training.

1

Progress

If the organization you have joined, or changed jobs within, is a forward-looking one that has a well-developed and well-established training and development department, you should be eased into your new job with care. A typical effective plan would include an induction period; observation of existing courses; early attendance on a train-the-trainer programme, either internally or externally; a planned developmental period; acting as second trainer with an experienced trainer on a training course (initially being the 'helper', but progressively starting to go 'solo' on some sessions or activities); until the day you become either a fully paired trainer or even the lone trainer on a course that has been running for some time; then the ultimate of being given a programme to plan, prepare, resource, implement, evaluate and develop.

But cases at the other extreme do exist in a number of organizations although hopefully they are few and far between. Here you might be thrown in at the deep end by the organization or a training manager who does not believe in trainer training! You could be given a minimum of preparation time, given existing scripts, briefs, handouts and training aids with which to work for an ongoing course, and told to get on with it! This must be the ultimate, albeit not the optimum in self-development, but it is certainly not the most effective preparation for a career as an effective trainer. If this happens to you, read this and other training books, watch videos and press hard to be sent on an early train-the-trainer course.

There will, of course, also be paths somewhere between these two categories.

Induction

Whatever the organization's attitude to the development of a trainer, most will look to you to introduce some aspect of managing your own development. Perhaps your employer has some form of induction programme that is designed to introduce you to and ease you into the job. Even if an induction programme is not available it is incumbent on you to find out as much information as you can about the job – its philosophies and practices, and the organization – its cultures and requirements. If you are left to your own devices, follow a traditional self-training approach – GAFO = Go Away and Find Out!

You will need some help in deciding what information you need unearth, in order to avoid wasting time. Many induction programmes include some aspect of GAFO and the following guidelines are typical of these. Hopefully, and this is usually the case, the people you approach will be willing to talk about their jobs, the organization and their place in it, their views on what is expected of you, and so on. You will receive some rebuffs – accept these and go and find somebody else who is more cooperative!

Induction guidelines

1. **The organization:** If one exists, obtain a copy of the organization chart (with names and responsibilities) and try to memorize as much as you can. Find out where the people and the sections listed are to be found.

2. **Senior management:** Find out the names and responsibilities of the senior management team – they will certainly have some contact with you at some stage and they will expect you to know about them. If they are approachable seek a meeting with them to obtain as much information and opinion from them as possible, particularly their views on training and development and the role of the trainer.

3. **Meet people:** Meet as many people in the organization as you can, concentrating first on those who will have direct contact with the training department – your training manager or senior trainer will advise you about them. But do not ignore the others, they could be future sponsors or clients of the training department and will appreciate this contact. When meeting people seek not only factual information, but their views and opinions, particularly about training and development – what they think of its effectiveness and cost, the major training needs for themselves and their staff and where they see you and the training department helping them.

4. **The training manager:** Hopefully you will have been welcomed by the training manager or, if there isn't one, by the senior (or other) trainer, or in some cases (where only this is available) by the manager in the organization who has a responsibility for the training department – you. It is often necessary to seek a subsequent meeting with this person to obtain, confirm or clarify your job description (preferably in written form), what the contents of this really mean; the views of the department about the philosophies and practices of training and development; what you will be required to learn and within what time period; what cultural or organization behaviours will be expected of you; and some indication of the learning process you will be following and how you will be helped along this path.

5. **Other trainers:** If there are other trainers in the department in which you will be working and with whom you will be associated, arrange to meet them as soon as possible. They will be able to tell you from the working

viewpoint how the philosophies, attitudes, behaviours and practices actually work in the department and give you a detailed description of your potential place in the scheme. They can tell you about the training programmes that are run and something about the learners who attend them. Particular information will be available about the programmes with which you will become personally involved and what they are hoping for from you. Cultural information about dress standards, attitude standards, etc, will be readily available from them. These are your immediate colleagues, with whom you will be working closely and relying on to a major extent, particularly in your early days, so get to know them as people, make friends with them and let them see that you are enthusiastic to learn.

6. **Training resources:** In your training duties, both when you are learning and when you are more experienced, you will need to make use of all available resources. Many larger organizations have resource libraries containing not only operational and training publications but also training and subject videos, CDs and CD ROMs, and also have computers and software programs for training/learning purposes. The computers will open up the world of the Internet and other CBT (computer-based training) facilities. The training department may also have computers linked to a network or intranet, which are used not only for internal communication but also in training programmes, where the learners remain at their workstations and log in to training over the Net. You will need to learn what these facilities are and how to use them effectively. The resource library may also be the recipient of management, industrial and commercial and training journals and magazines, some of which may need to have your name added to the circulation list.

It is here too that the information may be held about the pathways to professional recognition and advancement. It may be too early for you to take these steps, but it is useful to discover what is available and what you will need to do in the future, and indeed immediately, to avoid problems at a later stage. The current major professional recognition pathways are via the Training and Development National Vocational Qualification (TDNVQ), the Chartered Institute of Personnel and Development (CIPD), the Institute of Training and Occupational Learning (ITOL), Master's degrees in training and development (eg MEd, MPhil) via full- or part-time courses or distance learning and even the Internet.

For many of these qualifications you will eventually need to produce a personal portfolio of development and experience. Your induction or self-induction notes can form the first stages of this portfolio, so it is well worth retaining them for this purpose.

Although I am recommending obtaining what appears to be a mass of information, remember that you will not be expected to do everything at once – restrict your activities to those you can manage at present, but bear in mind future development possibilities. Also be warned that once you are in the full swing of training, you may not find the time or opportunity to take the action.

7.   **The training administration section:** The final group of people with whom it is necessary to make your initial contacts are the ones who are responsible for the administration of the training programmes in which you will be involved. These are the people, frequently in a separate training administration section or in the general clerical section allocated to training matters, who perform the thousand-and-one behind the scenes activities. They are the ones who call up the people to come on training programmes, print the handouts and often produce the trainer's training aids, and maintain all the files and other documents relating to the training process. Without an efficient back-up such as this, the trainer would have difficulty in finding time to do any training!

Get to know who and what they are, and in particular any specific people who will be responsible for the administration of any programmes in which you will be involved.

8.   **The organization:** If you are new to the organization an important step is to find out as much as you can about the work of the organization itself – products, services, etc. This information is essential in dealing with managers, supervisors and operatives, whether or not they are coming on training programmes, as you will need it when the time comes for you to help them with solving their training problems. Obviously, if your training is going to involve technical or clerical operations, you must start to learn as much as possible about these operations, having identified the ones that will be your priorities. You will have to learn about them and in some cases be able to perform them well, otherwise you will soon be in difficulties. Again the first stop is with the people actually performing the work – in the majority of cases they are the experts.

But the general action will require you to seek information about:

–   What does the organization produce or provide services in?
–   Who are its customers?
–   Is there a customer services policy?
–   Who are the principal competitors?
–   What processes or methods of service are used?
–   How are the products made?

  - How are the products or services delivered?
  - How successful is the organization?
  - Has it a published purpose plan or mission statement? Where is it?
  - Is the organization recognized under Investors in People?
  - How is the management of knowledge controlled?
  - How is quality measured and controlled?

And so on.

9. **How about a mentor?:** This could be a question to raise with the training manager – does the organization support the concept of mentors and, if so, are you to have one? The mentor will probably be from the training and development or human resources (HR) department, but not necessarily so.

   A mentor is an experienced person in the organization who has the motivation and commitment to help others develop, not necessarily a coach or trainer for you, but someone who can guide and advise you in your development. At a certain level, a mentor can open doors for you that might otherwise be closed. The mentor can be a guide for you during the first few months of your development or over a longer period until you are able to work fully as a developed individual. The mentor can:
   - regularly review with you your developmental plan and its progress;
   - identify relevant training programmes for you to attend;
   - agree resource materials for your progressive studies;
   - agree how you can be given feedback on your progress, by either the mentor or another observer of your practice.

10. **Health and safety:** In most organizations there is either a health and safety officer (HSO) or someone responsible for these duties, but the concept of health and safety in industry and commerce is that everybody has a responsibility for it. Meet the HSO and determine:
    - the health and safety policies and procedures in the organization;
    - how these relate in particular to training programmes attended by learners;
    - what your health and safety responsibilities are;
    - who are the key people in the health and safety procedures.

11. **Action planning:** In conjunction with your training manager or mentor integrate the elements of what you need to do into an action plan setting out your intentions, and use it as a progress and summary record. A useful format can be as shown in Figure 1.1.

WEEK	ACTION	PERSONS TO CONTACT	TIME NEEDED	TO BE COMPLETED BY
1				
2				
3				
4				
5				
6				

Figure 1.1 An action plan format

When you have completed each action reflect on what you have done and learnt and write up your findings for: a) discussion with your training manager or mentor; and b) retention for your own records or portfolio.

Always approach your new contacts with an analytical attitude, as frequently someone who is new to a situation (as you will be) sees things that may be wrong or could be improved that have not been noticed by the performer because of their familiarity with them.

Progressive entry to practical training

The progressive development of the new trainer has been mentioned earlier in terms of an ideal format operated by effective organizations to smooth the entry of the person to practical training. A common practice is for the new trainer to:

1. Meet the trainer with whom he or she is to be associated in training and discuss the training programmes, etc, as suggested earlier.
2. Sit in as a notetaking observer on several actual courses. The notetaking must be approached seriously and assiduously bearing in mind that 'one of these days I shall be the trainer out there!' The number of courses observed will vary with the organization and the urgency of the trainer's development, but the aim should be a minimum of two occasions – the first to familiarize the new trainer with the course and the second to let him or her get down to serious 'soon it will be me' observation.
3. When the new trainer has observed sufficiently, the programme format, brief materials, handouts and training aids should be studied, with practice in the use of the last of these.

4. If at all possible, this is the stage at which the new trainer should attend a train-the-trainer course that will reinforce training techniques; give practice in writing briefs, handouts and constructing training aids; give practice in presenting sessions and facilitating activities and discussions; and generally give the new trainer some confidence to place him- or herself at the front of a group.

5. The next step would be for the new trainer to be personally allocated several sessions of different approaches within the programme, but with the experienced trainer sitting in, principally to observe and give eventual feedback.

6. Following one or two occasions of partial training practice, if both the new trainer and the experienced one are to share the programme, a suitable division of labour should be worked out, the new trainer conducting sessions without the more experienced trainer.

7. The penultimate stage, if relevant, is for the new trainer to conduct a complete existing programme as the lone trainer.

8. The ultimate experience is for the now not-so-new trainer to be given training material to plan, prepare, develop, implement, review and redevelop as necessary for a training programme for which he or she would have responsibility.

The trainer as a learner

Before the embryonic trainer can become a trainer, helping others to learn, there is a lot that he or she must learn. This includes the techniques, methods, approaches, behaviours and skills of modern training and, in an organization that prides itself on its effective training establishment, the members of the training department will be expected to be skilled in most of these modern approaches. The amount of learning looming ahead of the tyro trainer can seem insurmountable, but the old adage of 'How do you eat an elephant? In bite-sized chunks' is by far the most effective approach to this mammoth learning task.

Learning to learn is an essential when there is so much to digest, and one of the major problems that is usually encountered is how to remember it all. The simple answer is that you can't, at least not in your head. Most people find that memory is aided and learning eased by writing down the learning pieces. There are numerous methods of doing this and a number of books have been published that can be used as references. I want to describe the Learning Log method here with two examples that are relatively simple in their concepts but can be of immense value in remembering and learning items as they are experienced.

The Learning Log

Every experience we have can be viewed as a learning experience, whether it is positive or negative in nature, and the Learning Log is an ideal vehicle for recording this learning as we progress. Many train-the-trainer programmes include it as part of the ongoing learning process within the programme, with the recommendation that it is continued beyond the programme. But I believe the new trainer is in a position to start learning from day one and it is from this point that a Learning Log should be constructed.

A log is a simple document that consists of one sheet of paper or, in the case of the more sophisticated versions, three sheets. The more professional document can be constructed by preceding the recording pages with a descriptive preface. Two examples of a Learning Log are included here as Figures 1.2 and 1.3. Figure 1.2 is the simplest form and consists of one sheet of paper on which ongoing thoughts and key points of learning are recorded.

Date . . .

Things I have encountered that I want to discuss

Things I want to know more about

Things I want to remember

Things to do

Figure 1.2 The ongoing Learning Log

The items to be entered will stem from the learner-trainer's meetings and discussions with the people recommended earlier in this chapter; they could equally result from occupational reading or from train-the-trainer and other training programmes attended. Time at the end of the working day, or otherwise, should be allocated to sit and reflect on the day's activities, to read the notes made at the time and to complete the Learning Log, summarizing the reflections into a meaningful, permanent record. The simple acts of reflecting and recording will not only produce the start of a progressive or ongoing Learning Log that can be referred to at any time, but will also reinforce in the learner's mind the key points of the learning

A more 'sophisticated' form of the log is shown in Figure 1.3. This consists of three sheets for each day or learning event, the first of which can be used during, for example, a training day or when you are otherwise in a learning situation to make notes of the points you wish to remember. At the end of the day or event review these notes, and on the second sheet of the log describe these selections in as much detail as you need to be able to recall them at a later date. On the third sheet describe, preferably with a priority rating, from your entries on the second sheet, what you are going to implement or otherwise take action on. This daily or event set of log sheets can be reviewed on a training course the following morning in a discussion group or at your leisure. It is recommended that, however completed, you should reread and reflect on your developing log at intervals. In this way your learning will be reinforced and you will be reminded of other learning and implementation intentions.

A LEARNING LOG

KEEPING A LEARNING LOG

The objective of attending a learning event is to learn something you can use. A complex event can contain a number of ideas, concepts, activities, etc, that you might wish to implement at work. It can be difficult, particularly over an extended period, to remember all that you considered, perhaps even some important points.
   A Learning Log:

- gives you a permanent document in which to record these ideas as they occur;
- helps you at a later stage to think about what you have experienced and learnt, particularly the key ideas you want to retain;
- helps you consider at leisure which aspects you want to implement and how you are going to do this;
- is a reminder for you about your intentions when you get back to work;
- is a permanent record of your progress and development and of what you have learnt.

If the other notes you may have taken and the handouts issued during the training programme are combined with this log you will have a full record of your training to which you can refer at any time.
   Your Learning Log should be completed frequently during the event – preferably during periods allocated for this purpose – or during the evening following the training day. Do not leave its completion any longer than this otherwise there is the danger that some useful and/or important ideas or learning may be lost.
   From your ongoing notes section, review and select the ideas, techniques, suggestions and activities that you feel could be important or significant for you.
   In the second section of the log describe these selections in as much detail as you need to be able to recall them later.

In the third section, preferably with a priority listing, describe, from your list in the second section, what you are going to implement or otherwise take action on:

- WHAT are you going to do?
- HOW are you going to implement or action it?
- WHEN and/or BY WHEN are you going to implement it?
- WHAT resources will you need?
- WHO can or needs to be involved?
- WHAT implications are there for effects on others?

THE CONTINUED USE OF THE LEARNING LOG

On the training programme

At the start of the day following the one for which you have completed your log you will, in a small group, be asked to describe the entries you have made. This presentation will:

- help you clarify your thoughts on the area presented;
- help you in the recall process;
- widen the views of the remainder of the group who may not have seen the implications of the areas you have highlighted;
- raise the opportunity for clarification of doubtful points.

As a continuous process

A Learning Log is not intended for use only on training programmes. We are learning all the time, in every type of situation, and a log can help us to capitalize on these opportunities. If you read a book and there are ideas that you want to remember and implement, enter these in the log. If, in discussion with others, ideas are suggested that you feel may be of use to you, remember them and enter them at the first opportunity. Keep referring to your log constantly to remind you of activities that you have not yet implemented.

Your line manager in his or her process of your continuing assessment will not only find your log entries valuable in assessing your development, but could be impressed by your intent and persistence.

Remember that, if eventually you decide to seek the award of the Training and Development National Vocational Qualification, this record can form a useful part of the portfolio you will need to produce.

DAY ONE

SECTION ONE

Sheet 1 of set of 3

RUNNING RECORD OF ITEMS OF WHICH YOU WISH TO REMIND YOURSELF

SECTION TWO

Sheet 2 of set of 3

DETAILED DESCRIPTIONS OF YOUR SELECTED ITEMS

SECTION THREE

Sheet 3 of set of 3

IMPLEMENTATION DECISIONS

(Repeated for other days or events)

Figure 1.3 Another form of Learning Log

2

What Is a Trainer?

The role of the trainer

The role (or roles) of the trainer can extend over a continuum ranging from the one extreme of the 'sitting with Nellie' approach to the other, where the trainer is a facilitator – guiding, advising, selecting, but rarely doing what is usually understood as 'training'. In different organizations, with different programmes, at different times, a trainer may be called upon to fulfil all or most of these roles, or may be restricted to one or, at the most, two. Training for the trainer may be a continuous process as new roles and approaches are introduced to him or her and the trainer must be aware of the varying demands of each new role and take the necessary development or self-development action.

Training functions

The word 'trainer' carries this wide range of roles and meanings and what follows is a brief description of the major roles you may be asked to carry out.

The workplace instructor

These are trainers who carry out most of their training in the workplace, either actually at the workstation with a single learner or with small groups, at times at the workstation and at others in a training room (frequently somebody's office!). Trainers should be skilled, experienced and efficient themselves in the operation or subject being taught (usually they have progressed from the operation level) but should also possess an interest and commitment to helping others learn and develop.

The simplest form of 'instructor' is found in the 'sitting with Nellie' approach. Originally this consisted simply of a new worker sitting beside a skilled worker, observing what was done for a period, then being put on to the operation line alone. This was far from the most effective way of training a new worker, and the essential development was that 'Nellie' was not only the skilled worker but also had the skill (inherent or learnt) to be a trainer. It has been found over many years that the most effective mode of instruction in these circumstances is the 'Tell, show, do' approach. The learner has the task or job described by the instructor, who then demonstrates what has been described by performing the operation, procedure or service, repeating these two steps until the learner appears to have a reasonable grasp of what is required. The learner then practises the operation, under the observation of the instructor, until both are satisfied that no further learning progress can be made. The learner then moves into the operational area to perform the real tasks, albeit still under the care of the instructor.

This is the more mechanistic area of the training process, as the learning usually covers operations for which there is a set procedure that the instructor needs to follow to the letter. This does not mean that instruction need be boring, monotonous or completely formal for either the learner or the instructor otherwise the role would be unacceptable to but a few.

The trainer/tutor

This is probably the largest category role in training and development, and 'trainers' need to have a wide range of knowledge about the subject or skill; knowledge about the many techniques, methods and approaches; and the skills of presenting these to learners so that effective learning takes place. Some trainers will need (or are required) to follow a limited approach of, for example, input sessions and discussions, whereas others may have the skill to, want to, need to and are encouraged to use a full range of methods – activities, discussions, videos, computer-assisted or computer-based training (CAT, CBT), and so on. In most cases the role of the trainer is to be 'in charge' of the training/learning all the time, he or she dictating to a large extent both what happens and the pace of these activities.

The facilitator

Training and development programmes in many organizations are moving away from the formal training course controlled by the trainer (although of course these will always be required when new learning needs to take place) towards events that are initially trainer designed and led, but which quickly develop into workshops in which the learners are given more and more responsibility and authority for the event. In such cases the role of the facilitator is to take a more apparently passive role, acting as adviser, guider (in a subtle manner) and provider of resources and services when asked to do so by the learners. So, in addition to the traditional skills of the trainer, the facilitator must have the much more intangible skills of helping people in indirect ways, knowing when to intervene (and when not to), and have a bulging toolkit of activities, videos, case studies, role plays, mini-sessions, etc, sufficient to satisfy the unforeseen demands of the learners.

The most difficult part of the role of the facilitator is usually when the learning group appear to have reached an impasse in their problem solving, or are going down what (to the facilitator) is obviously the wrong road. In such and similar situations the facilitator must be able to control a natural training urge of stepping in and 'helping' the learners. Rather he or she must be able to stand back and allow the participants to learn in a very effective manner by getting themselves out of the hole they have dug for themselves.

The internal consultant/adviser

The internal consultant (that is, a training expert who is an employee of the organization rather than an independent consultant brought in from outside the company) has moved away from being traditionally seen as someone in the training area. The internal consultant can for example tackle corporate or senior management needs through varied and extensive means. He or she can become involved in training needs identifications and analyses, in more individual tutorials or advisory roles with senior managers. He or she can search for and advise on wider development opportunities for individuals or groups, including educational as opposed to training openings, and be the repository of an extensive 'library' of information and views about training and development methods.

Obviously such internal consultants will need to have extensive experience and knowledge, possibly having been trainers and facilitators prior to taking up this post. They also need the ability to work with people who are frequently at more senior levels than themselves.

The trainer of trainers

Attendance on train-the-trainer courses has already been mentioned as part of the development of the new trainer, and obviously these courses will need to be staffed. Usually the staffing is by skilled and experienced trainers who frequently specialize in this form of training. It is demanding work, requiring considerable skill and expertise over a wide range of essential skills, methods, techniques and approaches to help somebody to learn. To a new trainer attending one of these programmes the trainers must be credible and acceptable and able to react to these requirements, as they are in a position to be seen as training role models, whether they are setting out to do this deliberately or not. Highly developed skills of observation and the ability to give feedback to the learners as they progress are required.

The training designer

This has been a developing training role over recent years, particularly in larger organizations with extensive training and development departments. Training events are ceasing to be isolated events and becoming complex and complete training packages, with courses and other types of approaches linked in a complete programme. The training designer identifies and analyses the needs of the learners and designs one of these total packages, which might contain a set of instructional briefs or scripts for a training course, along with the handouts and training aids; perhaps it might be or include a training audio cassette or video, instructions on the use of a purchased Internet training package, and so on, all accompanied by a trainer's guide to the package.

Or at a simpler level, from the training needs identification, the designer might design the broad structure of the necessary training, including the overall objectives, then pass this to the responsible trainer to produce the detailed programme.

The designer must have an extensive knowledge of the working of training and all the facilities that are available to ensure a balanced and effective programme. He or she must therefore know where to obtain materials and resources and ensure that these are available for the responsible trainer. The designer may even be responsible for modifying purchased packages to suit the organization and its particular needs and so must have wide corporate knowledge.

The e-trainer

This is one of the latest additions to the list of trainer roles, introduced with the gradual extension of the Internet and the suppliers of CBT packages through the Internet, and frequently carried out by means of the organization's own network or intranet. Few CBT or other Internet packages can stand completely alone, except perhaps those that are entirely for knowledge acquisition (some people prefer reading from a computer screen to reading from a book). Most packages, particularly those relating to the so-called 'soft' skills – interpersonal or social skills, people management, and other skills where the interrelationships of people are concerned – require the intervention or support of a live trainer. Much learning starts with the acquisition of knowledge or information about the constructs of a skill: the learners then need to practise the theory, usually within a group and supported by a trainer, with their practice being observed and given feedback. Or the subjects presented may need discussion on either a one-to-one or group basis or raise questions in the learners' minds that can only be answered by a trainer or other expert.

In some cases an actual 'live' trainer may not be necessary on the spot but, as suggested, in most cases some form of support will be necessary – in an accessible location, at the end of a telephone line or via e-mail.

The e-trainer must have complete knowledge, not only of the subject but also of the Internet package itself, and frequently is responsible for purchasing and allocating the package.

The role descriptions above are obviously many and varied and would not be immediately available to the new, inexperienced trainer, but experience comes or has to come quickly at times and role requirements may change. The roles described are not discrete, frequently overlapping and required more or less within a particular role. The questions posed to various people as suggested in Chapter 1 should give trainers a good indication of the likely future demands that might be made on them and enable them to include development of these roles in their progression plans. Consequently the variety of skills required by a trainer can range from limited presentation skills to a role requiring the full compass of skills. Some of the specific skills are described in the next section.

The knowledge and skills of the effective trainer

The role of the trainer is the sum of his or her knowledge and skills in the range of training for which he or she is or will be responsible. The following descriptions relate to the general skills required by a trainer, some more specific skills being additionally necessary with some of the roles described above.

The knowledge and skills can be summarized as:

- organizational knowledge;
- management and operational roles and functions;
- training knowledge and skills;

- programme preparation skills;
- sensitivity and resilience;
- people skills;
- commitment;
- mental agility and creativity;
- self-awareness and self-development commitment;
- sharing;
- credibility;
- humour;
- self-confidence.

This is a frightening list for the new trainer, but obviously full knowledge and skills will not be expected immediately. Some of these are integral people skills but many have to be achieved and developed over an extended period.

Organizational knowledge

As suggested in Chapter 1, the acquisition of knowledge about the organization and its integral parts will depend on whether the new trainer is also new to the organization or is a promotee/transferee from within. Whichever, it is essential that the trainer is aware of the organizational hierarchy, the company products and services, the policies, cultural requirements and internal politics, and the power structure, organizational procedures and regulations additional to those such as the Health and Safety Regulations. The trainer will lose credibility if he or she suggests approaches, methods, etc, that are inconsistent with the requirements or procedures of the organization.

Management and operational roles and functions

The areas of concentration will depend on those in which the new trainer will be operating. But as much knowledge as possible must be gained of roles, functions, skills, responsibilities, status, power bases and authorities of the people within the areas concerned. How much freedom of operation is allowed (encouraged?) and is there an organizational image, particularly at management level? What are the lines of reporting and the levels of resources available at different levels?

Training knowledge and skills

Knowledge of training must include familiarization with the academic and theoretical models concerned with training methods and concepts. There must be a wide knowledge of training techniques and skill developed in as many of these as possible; techniques, methods and approaches necessary to put these models into practice must be acquired, as must an appreciation of the most suitable occasions for which particular techniques are appropriate. Trainers are required, if only for the sake of their own development, to keep up to date with innovations in training, new models and techniques, and changing attitudes. There are many 'flavours' in training – flavours of the month, flavour of the year – and frequently 'new' models appear that are merely rehashes of existing ones, given a twist to suggest originality. A wide knowledge of training concepts gives the trainer the skill in deciding among these innovations and introducing them into his or her own training as/if appropriate.

Programme preparation skills

Although some organizations have the training designers referred to earlier, most trainers are required to research, design, plan and prepare their own training programmes. These requirements necessitate a range of skills in drawing together the material needed for the event: selecting the most appropriate material; putting it into a coherent, logical and progressive order; and arranging the 'sessions' in manageable chunks. The techniques and methods have to be decided on, as do the range of resources needed to make the programme presentation most effective. Most training programmes or needs can be approached in different ways and the trainer must decide which is the most suitable or appropriate in the circumstances, taking into account the subject, the learning population, the skills of the trainers involved, and so on.

Sensitivity and resilience

It is essential for trainers to be sensitive throughout a programme, both to the needs of the learners and to their reactions, behaviours and feedback – verbal and non-verbal. Commonly, however poor a trainer's approach may be, the learners do not verbalize their feelings and disappointments, but the sensitive trainer will be aware that something is wrong from skilled observation of the non-verbal signals being given. Once the trainer realizes that there is a problem(s), action must be taken to bring this into the open so that it can be resolved. There are many activities that can be used for this purpose. The most effective one I have used is, at the start of the training day, asking the participants to write down three words or phrases that describe their feelings at that time. If there are problems, more often than not these are expressed in the three words/phrases; if there are none you know you have given them the opportunity to raise them.

Sensitivity is also a feeling a trainer may have but, if the events can be viewed objectively, oversensitivity can be avoided. Many trainers over the years have felt very downhearted and even almost destroyed when given feedback about their training (personal or course-wise) that has been negative or discomfiting. This must be used as a learning process, avoiding a feeling of dismay, accepting the comments, particularly if the same ones are made by several people, and ensuring that the problems are resolved.

A trainer's success should not depend on influencing people by making friends – training is not a popularity contest! Some trainers become very dispirited if they do not become the most popular person in the group. Failure to be so can be a cause of stress for some, and this must be resisted. Not every training event will be a 100 per cent success, and I have known many trainers who have gone home at night and had a quiet cry. This is the time to say, 'I can cope with this. What is wrong and how can I resolve it?' Rarely does a trainer have sufficient time to prepare for a programme, accede to participants' requests, complete tasks out of training time and so on – resilience is necessary to overcome this problem and many others.

People skills

The principal practical purpose of a trainer is to transfer his or her knowledge, skills attainment methods, and so on, to the people who make up the learning group. A trainer must like people (although I have met some – unsuccessful ones! – who don't) and be able to communicate effectively so that the information is understood, remembered, and encouraging for the learners to act upon. People skills in a trainer mean knowing when to talk and when to listen; knowing questioning skills and how to use them most effectively; being a good discussion 'leader'; avoiding playing games with people or patronizing them; and, referring back to the comments above, giving feedback with sensitivity.

The trainer must always remember that he or she is in a position of power, a position not necessarily given by or accepted by the learning group. This power base must be used to assist, not try to enforce, learning, and to encourage the use of effective behaviours and attitudes.

Commitment

It should go without saying that trainers must be or become committed to the training concepts in which they are dealing and to the purpose of helping people to learn. An absence of this commitment becomes obvious to the learners in a variety of ways – lack of enthusiasm, ineffective preparation and presentation, lack of sincerity and so on – and results, unless the learners are very committed themselves, in a diminution of the learning. Programme participants will excuse many faults and failures in a trainer – as long as they can recognize the trainer's enthusiasm, interest in the subject and them, and commitment. However, the reverse will apply.

Mental agility and creativity

Training is a lively, active and reactive and constantly changing event. One skill in the successful trainer is the ability to 'think on one's feet' when the unusual occurs. As mentioned earlier, training does not stand still, and to keep up with all the developments, assess their value and implement the best, requires an enquiring and agile mind. If authority is passed to the learners the trainer must be sufficiently agile minded to able to react to unforeseen requests, comments and other changes.

Mental agility usually goes hand in hand with creativity, and if a training programme becomes an established one that has to be implemented time and time again, in order to avoid it becoming boring and laissez-faire, the trainer must constantly be questioning how it can be changed and improved, usually by means of creative techniques. Even learners nowadays are looking for and expecting different and creative approaches to help them learn, and the trainer may lose credibility if these expectations are not satisfied.

Self-awareness and self-development commitment

The state of a trainer, particularly a new trainer, must change, and change can only be effectively assessed by good self-awareness of existing and required skills and knowledge. Effective trainers must be aware of the level of their skills and whether anything should be done to increase this. They should also be aware of their value judgements and behaviours and the effects of these on their training; and aware of their attitudes to such aspects as racism, sexuality, colour, political and religious differences. If any of these are not what would be expected in the effective trainer, steps should be taken to control or modify them where training is concerned. There is nothing wrong with a trainer having personal views and attitudes about any of these areas, but negative views must not surface and intrude on the training.

Self-awareness helps in the identification of self-learning needs in terms of knowledge and skills. When these needs are identified the effective trainer takes the necessary action for them to be resolved by attending training courses, reading training books, using an Internet development program, and so on. Take the initiative rather than wait for your employers to suggest action – they do not do this! One big plus factor is that a self-developer is frequently seen by his or her employer as a high achiever – this can't be a bad thing.

Sharing

The effective trainer is rarely one who works alone deliberately, although it is sometimes forced on an individual. When working with another trainer, whether it is the new trainer with an experienced one or vice versa, care must be taken to develop positive relationships of trust, support and reliance. Even if disagreements occur these must not appear before the learning group until they have been resolved – in some cases they can be used as live examples of developing interpersonal relationships!

A benefit of a shared training programme is that one or more of the other trainers can sit in on one or more of your sessions, particularly when you are introducing a new subject or approach. In this way you can obtain professional feedback on your performance, sharing the process by doing the same for your colleagues.

Credibility

In order to be effective the trainer must have credibility with the learners as someone who has complete, up-to-date knowledge of the organization and the subject. Ways you can help to maintain your credibility include:

- exuding charisma (interest, enthusiasm, commitment and sparkle) even when your knowledge has some limitations;
- doing the same when you have extensive knowledge, even when this is the 50th time you have presented the programme;
- being seen as an expert or very experienced person in the subject;
- having effective training skills;
- having a behavioural pattern that does not offend the learners;
- having a willingness to demonstrate that you can and want to learn yourself.

Credibility is rarely lost if, when asked a question or for some resource you are not able to provide, you promise to find out the answer or provide the resource if possible – and you do so. But this must not happen too often or your credibility will decline to that of someone who has obviously not prepared for a range of requirements.

Even though you may be quaking inside, give off an air of confidence, as visible overtimidity and uncertainty tend to reduce credibility, as does publicly criticizing colleagues or people in the organization and denying individual and group needs and rights. If you promise to do something, do it.

Humour

The use of humour in training is a debatable subject, although there is considerable practical evidence that training is more effective when it is enjoyed by the participants, and an over-serious situation can be lightened by the injection of humour. This does not mean that the trainer should be an all-singing, all-dancing performer with an inexhaustible supply of jokes. A balance between an over-serious and light-hearted approach must be attained – the 'jokes' that are received best are those that are relevant to the subject. The trainer must demonstrate an ability to laugh at him/herself and avoid using the group as butts of humour. Something to be avoided is recounting an anecdote to a group, using oneself as the person involved, only to find a colleague has already used the anecdote using himself in the same way!

Self-confidence

Many of the trainer requirements mentioned so far can be resolved if the trainer has confidence in his or her ability to present the training and help the participants to learn. Confidence in training comes from knowing your subject thoroughly and to a level greater than that of the learners, but with the earnest desire to help them to reach the level of your knowledge and skill, or those of some other model.

But all this technical confidence can disappear when you stand up in front of a group and have to deliver a session. There is no easy way out of this, only experience, practice, and taking every opportunity to be the one presenting the material. It may never be fully resolved as far as you are concerned internally, but you will succeed as long as the image you outwardly present to the learning group is one of confidence. Sometimes it can even help to admit to the group how you are feeling, but recognize that there are dangers in doing this or doing it too often. At one time learners on a train-the-trainers course were advised,

...e, even when you are not!' I do not go along with this, and would ...sincere' with 'confident'.

It is completely natural for trainers, particularly inexperienced ones, to feel nervous when in front of a group. In most cases this nervousness soon disappears as you get into the swing of the session. Trainers need to start being concerned when:

- they stop having symptoms of stage fright, because this may mean that they are no longer concerned about the level of their performance; or
- the initial butterflies stay with them and even increase during the session, producing a less than effective performance.

In conclusion, trainer skill is not automatic. The vast majority of us have to work hard at it to overcome the pitfalls, but the development is always worth it when, at the end of a programme, you have the feeling and the proof that your participants have learnt as a result of the experience and you have helped them to do this.

Who is a trainer?

The mind of the newly appointed trainer will be buzzing with hundreds of questions, some of which will have been answered by the preceding material and the actions suggested. But other more general and personal, perhaps wilder questions will soon take on some importance, including:

- What will be expected of me?
- How will I satisfy these expectations?
- How will I deal with these potentially frightening learners?
- How do I want to treat them?
- How will they treat me?!
- Will I like them? Will they like me? Do I want them to like me?!
- How will I be seen as a person/a trainer/someone from 'the organization'?

'After all, I know nothing about being a trainer.' This thought is common, yet it probably is so wrong. Most of us have been to school, some to college or university, and it was there that we encountered many examples of the trainer, otherwise known as teachers, tutors, lecturers or professors. Later on many of us became learners ourselves, in either formal training programme groups or in more informal on-the-job situations with a practical 'trainer' helping us to learn.

In all the group learning situations there was somebody at the front of the group, telling us, asking us, teaching us, helping us to learn, directing us, suggesting to us, and so on. What are our memories of these people and what impact did they have on us at the time to which we can relate today? See if your answers correspond to any of these:

- One who talked without stopping from start to finish – how long that session seemed to be!
- One who told jokes every other minute so that in the end we lost track of the reason for the session.
- One whose sessions were so full of different approaches and training aids that the time just seemed to fly.
- One whose session was so full of different approaches and training methods that he got mixed up with what he was using, lost his place. . .
- One who was interesting and had some good material, but was oh so serious all the time.

Which ones: a) did you like; b) prefer; c) learn from? Which type would you prefer to be as a trainer yourself?

There are not as many trainer types as there are grains of sand on a beach, but because they are people this often seems to be the case. A number of researchers and practitioners have produced models of the principal training types with instruments that allow you to assess yourself. These may help you decide what kind of trainer you want to be, have to be because the organization says so, etc. In other words, *who* are you going to be in training?

The 'Townsend' model of trainer types

John Townsend (first published in *JEIT*, volume 9, no. 3, 1985 and republished in *The Trainer's Pocketbook,* Management Pocketbooks, 1985 onwards) proposed a three-dimensional model of trainer types. His three dimensions identified the types in low–high levels in trainer skills: competence; and concern for participants. This produced eight discrete types of trainer. (His later model presentation changed these somewhat, but I prefer his original definitions.) The model is presented graphically in Figure 2.1.

Although Townsend's trainer types may appear lighthearted in the titles, they nevertheless represent the principal attitudes and approaches for people found attempting training, whether this is the organizational role demanded of them or because of a personal preference. Perhaps the real mark of the 'professional

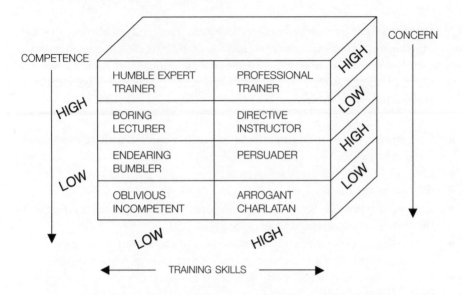

Figure 2.1 The Townsend model of trainer types

trainer' is his or her ability to take on some of the other roles when occasion demands.

The titles are self-explanatory and we have probably encountered most of them.

The oblivious incompetent is often the person who has been detailed to attend a training course as 'the expert speaker', even though he/she may not be so much of an expert and has virtually no training or presentation skills. However, oblivious incompetents are not aware of these failings, and usually nobody tells them, so they keep on in this mould.

The arrogant charlatan is rather similar to the oblivious incompetent except that in all probability he or she is aware of his or her failings, but hides them through a blustering façade of apparent skill and knowledge. Arrogant charlatans totally fail to consider the views and needs of their audience, who quickly see them for what they are.

The endearing bumbler is characterized by the absent-minded professor type who is obviously a subject expert but is so wrapped up in the subject that he or she has not taken the trouble to learn how to put this knowledge over. So endearing bumblers go bumbling on, wanting to help the group, but not really thinking about whether they are being successful.

The persuader is a master of training techniques and methods and uses these to persuade the learning group of the value of the messages that in many cases he or she has been told to present by the organization, whether agreeing with them or not. In many cases trainers who have been forced into this situation have only a limited knowledge or skill in the subject they are presenting, although they have the commitment to help the learners to learn. A difficult path to follow.

The boring lecturer is all too common, particularly in academic circles, but emerges in training events usually as the invited expert speaker. There is no doubt that they know their subject inside out and, with little concern for their method of presentation or to what extent they are helping their audience, they launch into the fullest detail of their subject. After about 10 minutes they have usually 'lost' their listeners and their whole session is a waste of time. A variation of this type with whom I have come into contact was a speaker on one of my courses, who overran his time by 20 minutes, setting back all the remaining sessions. He was told about this and promised to do something about it for the next time – and he did: he used exactly the same amount of material, but talked faster!

The directive instructor is usually a corporate instructor/trainer who has to ensure that the people attending the course (normally new entrants to the organization, to a new job or to take on new work) learn the subject so that they can return to work and operate. There is no argument that the participants have to learn, but because of the almost robotic manner in which the material is presented and with the unspoken, or even spoken, command 'Thou shalt learn', the command is difficult to obey, especially nowadays when learners are looking for a much different approach. The problem is that, when trainers have been in this mould for a long time (and for many years this was the acceptable training ethos), when a modified approach is essential they find it very difficult to adapt. One saying is 'Once an instructor, always an instructor'!

The professional trainer. This is perhaps the ideal level for all forms of training and one that most of us would love to achieve. 'Professional' is used in its widest, supportive sense, rather than the derogatory way in which it is occasionally used. Such a trainer has wide knowledge and skill in training techniques, methods and approaches; knows when each is most appropriately used; has considerable concern for the needs of the learners and tries to satisfy these needs, even by modifying the training material; can balance 'work' and 'social' times and does not become a 'Like me because I bought you a drink' trainer; has good people skills and can handle most situations effectively. The professional trainer has achieved the highest level when he or she can operate in this manner with little or no stress and everything is approached naturally. There is always the danger that professional trainers will become *too* good, or be seen as such, but this is less of a problem than with some of the other, less effective types.

Other trainer typology

The T–C training inventory

There are of course other models for describing the variety of trainer modes in which trainers might be required to operate, or in which they perform because that is their preferred method of working. A 40-question inventory (Pfeiffer and Jones (eds) in *The 1974 Annual Handbook of Group Facilitators,* University Associates, 1974) identifies the preferences of the completers of inventory in five training strategies. This is demonstrated in Figure 2.2. The 'T' stands for 'Trainee Orientation' and the 'C' for 'Content Orientation' and represent the trainer's attitudes towards the trainees or learners and the training content itself.

HIGH		
20	Strategy 2 That trainees do not really want to learn, but they will respond to trainers they like. The trainer's primary responsibility is to win trainees over so they can be taught	Strategy 5 That trainees, like all people, learn and explore. A trainer's primary responsibility is to integrate trainee and system needs by creating a learning climate and making learning meaningful and relevant.
15		
10	Strategy 4 That trainee and system needs are incompatible. It is of primary importance that something be taught, but trainee needs cannot be ignored. The trainer's first responsibility is to push them enough to get the work done but also to do something for them to maintain training session morale.	
0	Strategy 3 That trainees are lazy and indifferent to learning. Since a trainer is helpless to change the situation the primary responsibility is to present the information the system requires.	Strategy 1 That trainees do not want to learn, but they will respond to strong direction and control. A trainer's primary responsibility is to make sure the material gets taught.

T R A I N E E   O R I E N T A T I O N

0	5	10	15	20
LOW		**CONTENT ORIENTATION**		HIGH

Figure 2.2 The T–C training inventory

Trainer orientation framework

Another model, attributable to Andrew Pettigrew (*Guide to Trainer Effectiveness,* MSC/ITD, 1984), has a simpler questionnaire with only two polarized questions – this simplicity has raised questions about the effectiveness of the questionnaire, but the trainer types and their preferences are readily identifiable. The questions are as shown in Figure 2.3.

Where the point is located on the framework indicates the preferred trainer role orientation, but remember that the emphasis of the role will depend on your position within the quadrant (high up, low down, right or left).

The caretaker. Caretakers see the need for training to maintain the smooth running of present systems, procedures and technologies in the organization, and adopt traditional education and training approaches. They typically use trainer approaches that are trainer led, trainer centred and trainer controlled; they structure programmes highly and respond to training needs as presented to them by someone in authority.

The educator. Unlike caretakers, educators see the need for training to change systems, procedures and technologies, but like the caretakers tend to adopt traditional education and training approaches. They anticipate the need for change and work strategically by setting training objectives and designing and timetabling appropriate training programmes.

The evangelist. Evangelists see the need for training to maintain present systems, etc, but adopt a range of interventionist approaches. Basically they feel that traditional education and training approaches are inappropriate, and attempt to convert people in the organization to accepting a range of more learner-centred experiences in the form of, say, workshops, seminars and consultancy. They see their role more as an encouraging facilitator of learning than an expert on the subject matter and a traditional approach trainer.

The innovator. Innovators see the need for training to change systems, procedures and technologies in the organization, and adopt a range of interventionist approaches. They are particularly pervasive in the organization and aim to understand the real needs that exist. They persuade people to become involved and guide them through a problem-solving process rather than proposing solutions. In essence they are catalysts or change-agents.

Obviously there is no one right or wrong role, nor good nor bad, except if someone identifies with a role and finds themselves on the extremes of that role – for example, an evangelist with a vertical score of 1 and a horizontal score

1. Do you have an orientation to the maintenance needs of your organization, that is, to ensuring the continuance of existing activities, products or services? Or do you have an orientation to bringing about change in the organization, that is, to ensure training can respond to pressures for change from both outside and inside the organization to help it get geared up to meet new situations, objectives, etc? Mark on the scale below where you think you are.

Maintenance Orientation										Change Orientation
0	1	2	3	4	5	6	7	8	9	10

2. Do you have an orientation to traditional methods of training, that is, methods and approaches based on the 'educational' or professional model of training, based largely on classroom techniques and curriculum design? Or do you have an orientation to methods of intervention, that is, a 'change agent' approach to training that involves greater participation in bringing about changes in systems, procedures or technologies and in changing people's attitudes and approaches to work? Mark on the scale where you think you lie.

Traditional Educational Orientation										Interventional Orientation
0	1	2	3	4	5	6	7	8	9	10

3. Now transfer the scoring information from (1) and (2) to the framework below. Mark the place where the two points coincide.

```
                          Maintenance
                          Orientation

                               0
                               1
          Caretaker            2            Evangelist
                               3
                               4
Traditional  0  1  2  3  4     5  6  7  8  9  10  Interventionist
Educational                    6                  Orientation
Orientation                    7
                               8
          Educator             9            Innovator
                              10

                           Change
                          Orientation
```

Figure 2.3 Role orientation

of 10 would be an extreme example. Trainers with an extreme approach should ask themselves if they are performing good or bad work and whether their role should be tempered by aspects of the other roles. Indeed, the more balanced trainer will have the ability to take on, *where required*, any of the roles at the level needed. A singular approach must always be suspect, except in particular cases. But the trainer's role must reflect primarily the demands of the organization in which he or she is employed. There is little point in a trainer taking on the innovator role when the learning needs and the organization's culture demand an 'instructor' approach. If these demands are incompatible with the trainer's views, the trainer has several choices:

- to accept the organization's needs and adapt to the required role;
- to accept the organization's needs and adapt to the required role, but steadily attempt to introduce what he or she believes to be essential and acceptable changes to the organization and come nearer to his or her own orientation;
- to accept that unresolvable differences exist and seek employment in an organization with a more compatible culture.

3

The Input Session

In Chapter 2 you were introduced to the different types of trainer and training approach you might be called upon to perform once your initial induction and introduction to the training process and your role were complete. Whatever that role might be, at some time (probably sooner than later) you will be called upon to be the trainer in front of a group of learners with the purpose of presenting what I describe generally as an 'input session'. These sessions used to be called lectures, talks or presentations, but modern input sessions are rarely as stark as those terms suggest. Research by learning preference experts such as Andrew Kolb, and Peter Honey and Alan Mumford, has shown that learning is rarely achieved by trainees taking a passive role and sitting listening to a trainer, lecturer or subject expert talking at them for 30 minutes, an hour or, as used to happen, considerably longer.

The research shows that if effective learning is to take place, the learners follow the Learning Cycle. This is described with the initial action being an event of some nature, followed by the participants reflecting on the event, then considering the implications of that reflection, and finally, having learnt from the event and understanding all the implications, planning further action and implementing it. With this requirement for effective learning in mind, it becomes apparent that a trainer standing in front of a group and simply talking at them is not likely to be successful in helping the group to learn.

The basic approach

Although the singular approach of talking at the learning group is not recommended, in an input session where new information (that will later be translated into skills) is to be presented, a large proportion of the time will be taken up with a verbal presentation by the trainer. A basic part of the skills of the trainer is achieving mastery of presentation skills, or mastery as far as is possible. But before this the essential is knowing exactly where you are going in the session – planning and preparation.

The planning and preparation of an input session

As a new trainer, depending on the circumstances of training in the organization, you could be faced with one or more of the following circumstances:

- taking over an existing input session with a set of scripts and training aids;
- taking over an existing input session, but given the opportunity to customize the existing set of scripts and training aids;
- being given an input session with either new or to be revised material, in this case being expected to plan and prepare your own session and training aids.

In all these cases planning and preparation, to varying degrees, is essential. The degree depends on the type of session requirement.

Existing session (a)

In the case of taking over an existing session that you will need to present from existing scripts and aids, the preparation is basically putting yourself into a position to continue the session at its accepted level. You will need to:

- Read, familiarize yourself with and, if necessary, memorize the existing script for the session.
- Ensure that all the pages of the script are present and in the correct order.
- Ensure that all training aids are available, in correct order and, if electro-mechanical, in good working order.
- Ensure that all handouts and other paper aids are available and in good order.
- Familiarize yourself with the training environment and ensure that it is a) suitable and b) contains all the material you will require.

Existing session (b)

This may be a session for which you are given some responsibility in taking over its performance, but after you have looked at the material and modified it to suit your own training approaches. This may be as simple as editing the script and training aids to put them into a format that is more in line with the way you express yourself and the training information. To be able to do this you must by this stage have some knowledge and skill in the planning and preparation of training sessions from an existing base.

Planning a new session

This approach to an input session requires that you have by this stage some experience in performing the more basic input session, and also in planning and preparing a session from zero base. You will not of course be starting from absolute zero since you will be given the results of an analysis that has identified a training need of a particular nature that your session will satisfy (or it will be part of a relevant training programme). You will also be given guidelines on the time available for the session and on the range of material from which you should select for your session.

Otherwise the requirements will be similar to those listed earlier, but with additional elements:

- Determine the range of material from which you will decide your session.
- Identify the content priorities (see later).
- Decide on the type of session approach you will take – presentation, discussion, buzz groups, case studies, activities, etc.
- Write a session plan and session script, plus, if required, an abbreviated brief from which you will work during the session, taking account of the training approaches on which you have decided.
- Fully familiarize yourself with and, if necessary, memorize the script for the session and ensure the pages are in the correct order.
- Decide which training aids you will need for the session and prepare them or have them prepared. Ensure that all training aids of an electro-mechanical nature will be available and in good working order.
- Prepare and have printed all handouts and other paper aids.
- Familiarize yourself with the training environment and ensure that it is a) suitable and b) contains all the material you will require.
- Practise your presentation, preferably with a 'critical' audience who will give you constructive feedback. Otherwise practise your presentation, as far as possible, in front of a full-length mirror, recording the practice with an audio or video recorder. In the latter case the practice can be held in the room that will be used for the session.

In all these approaches, in addition to the guidelines summarized, you will need to develop satisfactory presentation skills so that you can help the learners achieve the maximum amount of learning from your input. This is a major subject in itself and trainers can help themselves to develop skill by reading the many books on the subject, attending training programmes on the subject (an essential of these is that sufficient time is allowed for more than one practice and feedback), listening to other trainers presenting, self-practice as mentioned above, but, above all, taking every opportunity to make a presentation, however frightening this might seem. As far as I know, nobody has ever died as a result of giving a presentation!

Presentation skills

This is a wide-ranging subject, including not only the verbal skills of the presenter but also non-verbal skills, using a range of approaches, knowing the audience (and of course the material), and all the technical aspects associated with the session.

Input sessions have their opponents, and their arguments are usually easily upheld when:

- the presenter has low skills in presentation;
- the presenter has obviously prepared the material badly;
- the material may not all be relevant to the subject and the learning group;
- the material is presented in an unorganized way;
- the session contains too much or too complex material for the group to readily assimilate;
- the session consists only of the presenter talking, with the group being expected to sit passively and learn from this approach.

The demands on the trainer undertaking an input session are not all one-sided – the audience also have a part to play, particularly if they are given an active rather than a passive role. But even the most skilled, entertaining and informative presenter is not assured of success if the group are not interested, committed and motivated to learn. Much of this can be developed by the trainer during the session, but there may be more basic undercurrents – the learners may have been forced against their needs and wishes to attend; individuals may have personal agendas; individuals may have overpowering personal problems from which they cannot divorce their minds; or they may dislike the trainer for some reason so that they force themselves not to learn!

Advantages and disadvantages

In addition to the potential problems described above, input sessions have advantages and disadvantages, all of which can be manipulated by the trainer to ensure the best effect. Naturally, much hangs on whether the input session is used: a) appropriately and b) in an appropriate manner, appropriate situations including:

- a general introduction to the subject;
- where there is a need for descriptive learning;
- the introduction of completely new material;
- at the early stages of a training programme when the learning group is insufficiently mature to cope with much participation.

More inappropriate situations would include:

- when the learning group has demonstrated a strong need to be active;
- when the subject is familiar to the participants and sharing their various experiences is likely to be more productive;
- where the training event is more concerned with people skills and behaviours than with technical processes.

Advantages

The trainer is in control of the material. This is the situation where the trainer decides what has to be included in the session and presented to the participants to learn, how it is to be presented, and follows these lines resolutely. Problems here are when the material is not what the group are expecting/wanting/needing and they want to raise questions and disagreements but are not allowed to do so.

The trainer is in full control of the time. In highly structured training programmes time is at a premium, each participating trainer being allocated specific periods of time for the sessions for which he or she is responsible. Failure to comply with this has a knock-on effect on the following sessions, but compliance illustrates that the trainer has good self-control and has prepared the material to fit the time allocated. The advantage is that the planned material (often essential) is covered, but it allows no latitude for a more active learning group that may want to discuss, question, disagree, etc.

The material can be covered in a logical order. In most cases the most effective form of presentation of material is logically, moving from the known to the unknown, rather than the presentation (albeit interestingly) of information in an unorganized manner.

A safe approach. Because the trainer has (hopefully) prepared the material well, in a relevant order, with necessary safeguards to avoid overrunning, he or she should then feel as far as possible in control of the session and therefore in a relatively safe position. Control and organization of this nature will not get rid of butterflies at the start of the session, but will ensure that they are kept to a minimum and are capable of further control as the session progresses.

Ease of trainer replacement. Occasions arise when the original trainer is unable to take an imminent session. If the session has been effectively structured, documented and arranged it becomes an easier task for a replacement to step in. This is not always the case in other training approaches that have not the structure and form of the input session.

Student safety. This is a rather suspect advantage, but in a completely formal input session the trainer has control, is the active person, and little demand is made on the group other than to sit and listen and take what learning they can. Previous comments suggest that, although this may be safe for the participants, they may actually achieve little learning.

Disadvantages
Where there are advantages in any situation there are generally also disadvantages. The input session is no exception and here the following might be included:

The presentation is ineffective. As has been commented on several times, the input of material may be an ineffective form of learning for a variety of reasons. For example, the session may be taken by a poor speaker with a boring, uninteresting, even 'offensive' manner that does not encourage the learners to listen, even though the material itself is essential and important to the learners. The learners themselves (as has been suggested) may make the session ineffective if they do not have the requisite listening skills or are not prepared to use them.

Repetition. There is a danger in any teaching or training situation, where the same session has to be repeated over and over again, that presenters who feel they have found what is (to them) a satisfactory formula for the session repeat it in the same way every time. The material may not in fact change over time (although the possibility that it might must be kept in mind), but the trap in the path of apparent success may not be evident to the trainer. He or she may become blind to a lack of sparkle in the presentation and the changing needs and attitudes of the learning groups. The result is that the session becomes less and less effective.

The session remains a trainer-presented, passive event. Learners nowadays are accustomed to and demand a varied approach that offers the maximum opportunities for their involvement, leading to more learning. A simple 'lecture' is doomed to failure in the training environment and must be varied with the range of other training tools now available.

Lack of feedback. When the learning group is passive and discouraged from making contributions there can be little or no feedback to the presenter on the success of the session, usually when it is too late. If the session has not succeeded, the planning, preparation and presentation energy will all have been wasted, a fact that may not be known to the presenter who may, as suggested above, repeat this 'failure' with another group. The apparent non-verbal signals given by a group of people can be completely misleading in considering feedback. A group sitting with pleasant looks on their faces, even smiles, and an air of attention, may indicate the complete reverse, the individuals hiding behind these façades to cover other thoughts.

Techniques for making the input session as effective as possible

The training input session can be improved to become effective principally by the use of two techniques:

1. improved verbal and non-verbal presentation;
2. the use of a range of training and learning techniques rather than the straightforward 'lecturing' approach.

The methods of (2) will form later chapters of this book, but much can be achieved by ensuring an interesting and effective presentation.

Presentation skills

Speaking in front of a group of people can be the most frightening experience in many people's lives. Fortunately trainers are given many opportunities to do this, and the more opportunities they have the less frightening it becomes. Nerves immediately prior to and at the start of the event never disappear completely; but this is advantageous, since if presenters are not afflicted with butterflies it almost always suggests that they are not concerned about the success of the event and the needs of the group. This lack of concern would almost certainly be reflected in the value of the event.

Butterflies

So, butterflies are not only natural, but they are almost desirable. Obviously if their effect is very severe this can have an adverse effect on the event, but there is usually an identifiable reason why this is the case. Most often the cause can be traced to insufficient planning and preparation leading to uncertainty about presenting the material. It may be oversimple to suggest that, if the presenter is completely sure of the material, how it is to be presented and how the session is to be run, the butterflies may reduce considerably. They rarely disappear completely, even when the presenter has performed the same session several times. Experience of the majority of trainers confirms both these opinions.

In addition, there are some aids that can be used, including:

- While you are waiting to start speaking, take several deep breaths, as unobtrusively as possible.
- Whatever rehearsal you have prior to the event, rehearse the opening part until you are word perfect. You will find that once you start speaking confidently the butterflies will start to settle down.
- Clench and unclench your fists (out of sight!).
- Speak more slowly than you usually do, otherwise you are likely to gabble.
- Even if you are going to sit down during the presentation, stand up at the start, introduce yourself and the subject, then sit down.
- Start with the simple things before moving on to complex arguments.
- Don't sit behind a table, as the barrier it represents keeps you apart from the group and inhibits the development of an easy relationship. But do not sit on the edge of a table as inevitably you will swing your legs, an action that frequently: a) encourages nervousness, and b) makes any nervousness obvious (swinging/moving legs and feet suggests that the owner wants to run away!).

The effective control of session time

One factor that introduces nervousness in the session presenter is fear of: a) overruning the allocated time and b) within this time not putting over all the material to be presented. Several techniques can be employed to get rid of these fears.

First, ensure that there is a clock at the back of the training room that you can see easily. This is much more effective and less obvious than having to keep looking at your watch on your wrist or even on the table – you are already looking in the direction of the group and looking round them, so a movement of your eyes to the clock will not be obvious.

The second technique is to use a method that has been employed successfully for many years – the Must Knows, the Should Knows and the Could Knows. When you have collected all the material in the planning/preparation stage that you feel should be included in the session, look at it critically and divide it into three categories.

The Must Knows will represent the material that must be included effectively in the session and has the highest priority for the time. You will have no excuse for not putting over any of this material.

The Should Knows include the material that is important, but not to the same extent as the *Musts*. If during the sections of your session (and you should in your preparation have identified how long each section should take) you find that you are short of time for a section, you can omit some of the *Should Knows* to catch up.

The Could Knows, although interesting and useful for the learners to hear about, are the items that, if they were excluded, would not have a major effect on the learning from the session. If time is running short and the *Must Knows* and some of the *Should Knows* are in danger of being crowded out, drop the *Could Knows* – however interesting you think they are and however much the learners would like to hear about them.

Before the start of the input session

Before your actual session you will need to make a number of decisions (if this is allowed you) when preparing your session script or brief.

Selecting the appropriate approach

One of these decisions might concern the approach to the session you feel will be the most appropriate. This obviously requires extensive knowledge of the approaches and techniques available, of which you as a new or fairly new trainer will not yet be fully aware. However, you will have resources (other trainers, etc) available to help you in this. As a start, the following summarizes the factors you will need to take into account.

The content

- Is the session content knowledge, skills or attitude and behaviour changing, or a mixture of these?
- Is the material of a technical, operational, general or specific nature?

The audience

- Do you have any knowledge of the audience's learning method preferences – activist, reflector, theorist, pragmatist? (Refer to Honey and Mumford's *Learning Styles*).
- What knowledge do they have of the subject?
- What experience do they have of the subject?
- How many people will be in the group and what is their status in the organization?
- To what extent have their needs been identified and analysed?
- How common or diverse are the needs in the group?
- What expectations have they?

Some of these factors may be difficult to determine and some may need to wait to be identified at the start of the training event.

Available resources

- What is your experience of the subject? Is this relevant?
- What is the extent of your knowledge of the subject? Do you need to extend this so you can cope with any problems or questions from the group?
- Are you the lone trainer or is there other trainer support?
- To what extent are training aids available?
- How much time have you available: a) for preparation, b) for the event?
- What are the environmental factors?

The organization

- What end result does the organization expect of you and the event?
- Does the organization have preferred methods of training and/or presentation?
- What are the traditional attitudes accepted in the organization?
- Does the organization have a progressive attitude?
- What are the demands on the trainer as presenter – dress, appearance, manner, attitude?
- What are the validation and evaluation requirements?

The sequencing of material

The need to ensure an appropriate sequencing of material throughout the event has already been mentioned and movement in a logical progression has been recommended. However, there are other sequences that can be followed, the selected one depending on the nature of the material to be presented and the most appropriate method.

The alternatives include:

- from the known to the unknown;
- simple to complex;
- easy to difficult;
- logical stepping in a process;
- interesting material to more serious needs;
- random sequencing;
- dependency on a pattern of sessions to determine the learning;
- knowledge to doing;
- doing to knowledge to doing.

Session planning

Before starting on the preparation of a working script or brief, it is useful to prepare a session plan that, without going into the detail of the brief, describes the proposed content of the session and can include stage directions to the use of the 'Knows' and the training aids anticipated.

A session plan for a Presentation Skills session is shown in Figure 3.1.

The session brief

The next stage prior to the event is to prepare the script or brief that you will use during the session. I prefer the term 'brief' to 'script'. 'Script' suggests a fully written out session that appears to be a memorized speech or a set of sheets from which the session is read out. Both of these are mechanical and lifeless and should be avoided. By all means write out the session in full when at the planning stage, but do not use it during the session.

Rather think in terms of using a 'brief', that is, a set of notes that are as brief as possible taken from the full script. The most common form of brief is the 'Headline' method, a variation of and modification from the full 'essay type' script, which involves cutting out many of the words from the full script and making the resulting brief a document that can be used and referred to easily during the session. The three stages of construction are:

List headlines on A4 sheets

Identify the main subjects of the topic and list these as main subject headings, leaving space for relevant text below each heading. When preparing the brief it is useful to make a first draft, with spaces between each heading so that the headlines can be moved around when the most appropriate order has been determined.

SESSION PLAN FOR A PRESENTATION SKILLS SESSION

	Approximate timing
1. Introduce the session and describe the session objectives and methods, particularly any specifics. Seek group's experience of making presentations.	10 minutes
2. Give input session concentrating on the skill attributes of session presentation. Include attention span and barriers to communication.	20 minutes
3. During input session, when communication barriers are being introduced, form buzz groups to identify possible barriers and solutions to them. Take feedback from the groups and display OHP summary slide, adding ideas from the groups.	20 minutes
4. Group members to present their 10-minute sessions (previously arranged) – two groups of 4 = 4 × 10 minutes plus 4 × 10 minutes review of each presentation. Add discontinuity time (20 minutes).	1 hour 40 minutes
5. Final review and roundup session	15 minutes
Total session time	2 hours 45 minutes

Figure 3.1 A sample session plan

Enter inter-heading summarized notes

Under each main subject heading enter summary notes relating to that heading. These notes should be as brief as possible for ease of reference, but sufficient to enable you to develop the subject from them.

Edit the brief for final content

The material can now be edited by annotating the margins with comments on the Must, Should and Could Knows; adding stage directions, such as the use of training aids; and approximate timings.

The session brief working copy

The actual working brief can be copied as a final draft on to A4 sheets of paper or large index cards, individual sheets or cards being used, as desired, for each main heading. Colours can be useful in dividing the key points or identifying particularly important areas, or even for stage directions. The colour range should be kept to a minimum otherwise you will forget which colour means what!

Numbering the pages or cards is essential as you may, as time goes on, extract sheets to amend them, or it is not inconceivable that you might drop them, even during a session! To avoid problems in the latter case, always tag the sheets or cards to hold them together.

There is no golden rule about the use of the brief during the session, except that that you must have it available, whether or not you actually use it. You will certainly need to use it during the session in your early days of training, but as your skill and experience increase and you become fully aware of the session, you might not need to refer to it. However, even experienced trainers always have their brief with them for reference should the need arise (memory can fail!).

Many trainers say that they feel self-conscious about using their notes during the session in front of the group. If you lay the brief on a table to your side, glance at it and turn the pages over as necessary, this is not as obtrusive as you may think and, even if the group notices what you are doing, they will usually not react badly. It is better to ensure an effective and flowing session, even if you are seen to be using your notes, rather than flounder and fail because you want to avoid being seen using them.

The training environment

You may not be given any options about the location, size, shape, etc, of the environment in which you will have to present your input session, but you should certainly obtain the answers to some critical questions well before the event, particularly if the environment is strange to you.

Figure 3.2 lists the questions you should ask about the training environment and other things prior to the event.

Some trainers, usually the more experienced ones, claim that the environment does not affect their presentation skills, but, particularly in your earlier stages, you are advised to take notice of this factor. In many cases, of course, you will not have the opportunity or the authority to modify it in many ways, but if it is going to make you feel more comfortable in your session, try to get the environment as suitable as possible for you and your learning group. Uncomfortable locations inhibit both your presentation and also the listening and learning capabilities of the participating group.

Barriers to effective training environments exist and you should be aware of these – Figure 3.3 lists the major examples. Notice that some of the barriers may actually be benefits!

ENVIRONMENTAL AND ALLIED QUESTIONS

- How large an audience will there be?
- How big is the room?
- To what extent is this size going to affect the extent of my vocal presentation? How loudly am I going to have to speak to be heard at the back of the room?
- What will the nature of the event be? (The amount of interactivity will have a major effect on the layout and audience intervisibility.)
- Will discussion be involved?
- Which type of visual aids are going to be: a) possible, b) the most effective?
- Which aids are provided and are they satisfactory (modern, working) or do I need to take my own?
- Where am I going to place the visual aids equipment: a) flipchart, b) overhead projector, c) video monitor, etc?
- Can the visual aids be seen by all of the audience?
- Where, how many and what type of power points are available?
- (In conjunction with the size of the audience) can I sit or stand?
- Will I be required to sit behind a desk or stand behind a lectern? (Avoid this if at all possible.)
- Is there any chance of moving these?
- Will I be using a brief, OHP transparencies, handouts?
- Will there be a suitable location to place these items?
- Are there alternative places to put: a) my brief, b) my OHP transparencies, c) my handouts?
- Will movement be impeded in any way?
- Will I be easily visible from all parts of the audience?
- What is the seating arrangement?
- Is this the most effective?
- Can it be modified in any way? Permanently? For buzz group event, etc?
- Is there a visible clock in the room?
- Where are the toilets?

Figure 3.2 Environmental and allied questions to ask

What to do immediately prior to the event

The environmental and allied aspects will have been cleared by you as suggested above at a reasonable interval before the training event, but there are other actions to take and questions to ask immediately prior to your event, before you arrive at the training room. Some of the items to check are included in Figure 3.4.

SOME BARRIERS TO AN EFFECTIVE ENVIRONMENT

Room too large	May overpower a small group
	May inhibit discussion/participation
	May prevent participant/speaker rapport and interrelationships
	Small group may feel lost in the large space
	May be required to have an undesirably larger group
	Maintains formality and remoteness
Room too small	Participants might feel claustrophobic
	Personal space may be cramped
	Size of group restricted
	Forces a close group/speaker proximity
Pillars in large room	Will restrict vision
Lighting	If too low/too high can disturb group's comfort
	Too-low light prevents notetaking
	Inhibits intervisibility if too low
Tables	Can be seen as barriers between the trainer and the participants
	Barriers to movement
	Restrict placement of audience
	Materials might pile up untidily
Irrelevant decoration and retained posters	Give an unprofessional appearance
	Can interfere with attention
Glass doors, windows – external and internal	Movement visible outside the room can interfere with attention
Platform	Makes speaker remote from audience
	Reduces speaker/audience rapport
Lectern	Implies speaker superiority
	Acts as barrier between speaker and audience
Intervisibility for group members	Essential for certain types of events, not for others

Figure 3.3 Some barriers to an effective environment

A presenter's toolkit

In spite of all the checks you will have made, including immediately before the event, Murphy's Law says that if anything can go wrong it will! So many trainers go to an event personally prepared but with a toolkit containing items that they know may not be available or do not work. I would recommend that you construct a small but efficient toolkit (though you can't be prepared for

- Do you have with you the relevant brief?
- Do you have with you all the relevant visual aids?
- Is the relevant visual aid equipment available?
- Does it all work correctly?
- Is replacement equipment readily available if required?
- Is the seating layout as you wanted, or the best available?
- Can the visual aids be seen clearly by all the audience?
- Is there a clock easily visible by you? If not, you will have to take your own.
- If relevant, are tables provided and are there writing materials?
- Are refreshments provided for you and the audience? If so, have the arrangements been confirmed?
- Have the room temperature and ventilation arrangements been made and working?
- Are all the other room arrangements satisfactory?
- Do you know who to contact in case of problems, and where the people are to be found?
- Are the administration staff aware of the interruptions policy?
- Have any changes occurred since the original check?

Figure 3.4 Checks to make immediately prior to the event

everything) to take with you to all your events. Experience will show what further items you need to pack. Here are a few ideas:

- at least one pack or pad of paper, A4 or A5, whichever you normally use or require;
- a pack of blank index cards, small and large;
- pens, pencils, dry-marker pens, marker pens, Lumocolour pens (water- and spirit-based);
- masking tape and other adhesive tape;
- Blu-Tack;
- stapler and box of staples, paper clips, Post-it pads, scissors, ruler, erasers;
- calculator;
- diary and address list.

Plus, as required if in residence at the training accommodation:

- change of clothes – in addition to a normal change, have a spare shirt/blouse to change into during the day, and also your 'working clothes' into which you can change before the event if you have had a long journey in casual clothes;
- toiletry items.

The time is approaching when you are going to have to present! But there is still some work to do. This is discussed in Chapter 4.

4

How Do I Get Them to Listen?

The material you have planned and prepared as suggested in Chapter 3 may be the most valuable and interesting material you can find, but if your presentation itself is monotonous, uninteresting in the way it is presented, unenthusiastically presented and so on, there is a very strong likelihood that little or no learning will be achieved. An effective presentation requires not only good material but also an effective presentation by you. Variety of approach is also required, but we will look at that in the next chapter, so here we shall concentrate first on you, the speaker. Very few of us are born speakers, so the majority have to work hard at developing presentation skills to ensure that we are not wasting the value of the material we have. A number of tips and guidelines will be given in this chapter, but, and I offer no apology for repeating this again – practice on as many occasions that you can.

Every good presentation, session or discrete section of a session has three stages – the opening, the main body of the presentation, and the ending. Each has some specific techniques to ensure success (or at least approach it). Let us start, naturally, at the start.

Opening a presentation or session

Some specific techniques that you can use at the start of the session include:

- control the butterflies;
- write down your first sentence or two;
- be sure of your introduction and how you are going to make it;
- don't apologize;

- start with a bang – grab their attention;
- after your introduction, pause to encourage attention;
- describe the framework of the session, particularly if it is going to contain several approaches or is particularly complex;
- tell them what you are going to tell them about;
- define the questioning strategy;
- set the mood – use humour, ask a question to start involving them;
- start involvement with a short introductory or icebreaking activity;
- seek expectations.

Most of these are common sense and require little explanation. The control of butterflies and writing down and memorizing your opening words has already been mentioned. Other techniques listed include the following.

Introductions

Are you going to be introduced by someone or are you going to do this yourself? In the former case, have written down what you would like this person to say and agree this with him or her. Otherwise, consider what you are going to say – self-introductions should be planned and should be as short as possible, with the aim of letting the group members know who you are with some attempt to establish credibility and authority. Be careful not to appear to be boasting as this could antagonize some members of the group from the start!

A different approach is to use a visual aid, for example an overhead projector slide, showing (preferably graphically and, if possible humorously) something about yourself. This technique can be particularly useful if you are going to ask the group to introduce themselves in a similar way.

Apologies

Never apologize at the start of the session, for example by saying that this is your first session – the more you apologize the more credibility you could lose, rather than gain sympathy! Why are you apologizing? It should certainly not be for your material and you have prepared yourself to give as good a presentation as you can at this stage in your career. Don't apologize for lack of preparation time – the group might feel that this is an insult to them. Go into the session and enjoy it.

Start with a bang – grab their attention

A very large proportion of the success of your session will be the result of your catching the group's attention from the start and, of course, maintaining this attention. Start in a positive or an impactful way, doing or saying something to which they can relate. But beware of going over the top with this, as too revolutionary a start could for some people in the group be a turn-off or even an insult. When you have more experience you will be able to assess when you can be gimmicky or controversial.

After your introduction, pause to encourage attention

This helps you to slow down the start of your session, as mentioned in the previous chapter. The pause helps you to pull yourself together and realize that you have managed to start. It also tells the group that the introduction is finished and that you will soon be starting on the real meat of the session. There is no golden rule about how long the pause should be – any length of pause will always seem longer to you than it will to the listeners and it can act as a spur to their preparing to listen.

Describe the framework of the session, particularly if it is going to contain several approaches or is particularly complex
Tell them what you are going to tell them about
Define the questioning strategy

Groups like to have a map laid out for them of what is going to happen – this could be a verbal map or a poster with the session paths outlined. Describe briefly not only the stages you will be following, but also a brief summary of what will be included. A well-established approach during a session or presentation is, to 'Tell them what you are going to tell them. Tell them. Tell them what you have told them.' If the subject lends itself, a leaf can be taken out of a sales approach by, in addition to telling them about the material, describing the benefits to them.

You can determine what questioning strategy you are going to follow during the session and information about this should be given to the group right at the start. The decision is not a simple one. If you decide that you will only accept questions at the end, by the time this arrives the potential questioners may have forgotten what they were going to ask or, during the session, be disgruntled that they cannot ask when they want to do so. On the other hand, if you allow questions at any time there may be a number of interruptions that could throw your timing out significantly, although you are letting the group know that you are willing to react to them.

A possible compromise is to stop at the end of obvious sections of the material and have a question period on those sections. You need to build in time for this in your preparation.

Set the mood – use humour or a quotation, or ask a question to start to involve them

Humour

The approach will be determined by the type of subject. Obviously if the subject is a very serious one humour at the start could be out of place, but otherwise a humorous or light-hearted approach will let the learning group know that the session will not be too 'heavy'. Be careful – humour is a difficult approach to take successfully; one person's humour is not another's. One caveat is 'Don't just tell a joke. Make it relevant.' – the group may not understand it; they may not find it funny; they might think 'What has that got to do with anything?'; it may offend for a variety of reasons. Are you good at telling jokes anyway?

If you do start with a joke or other humorous comment make sure that it is appropriate and directly related to the subject, eg something that happened to you in the situation to be discussed.

Some people have a natural sense of humour to which others readily respond – if this is you, use this facet in your approach.

Use a quotation

Quotations have virtually the same caveat as humour – they must be relevant and add something to the opening. Some guidelines are:

- Keep it short.
- Ensure that it is relevant and appropriate to the subject and/or the group.
- Ensure that the group will understand it and can relate to it.
- Let the group know why you have repeated the quotation and the import-ance of the person making it, eg a quotation from the chief executive may carry more weight that one by Shakespeare. But beware of changing priorities – surveys are currently reporting that Bart Simpson is quoted more frequently that Shakespeare!
- If the quotation contains more than half a dozen words, consider putting it on a visual aid rather than simply saying it.

Ask a question

Asking the group a question in the opening stages can serve a number of purposes:

- It gives you something to say to start the session!
- It lets the group know that you want to involve them and that the session is going to be interactive.

- It tells the audience that you are interested in communicating with them and hearing their views, rather than just talking at them.

As with humour and quotations, however, the question must be relevant to the topic or situation. A simple one might be, 'Can anybody not see the visual aids?' or 'Can anybody at the back not hear me?' (These questions are framed in a more effective way than asking if everybody can hear/see, which might get no response, and that in turn means nothing; whereas no response to the more specific question should mean that all is satisfactory.)

If the questions relate, for example to the extent of the group's knowledge or attitudes to the subject, ask questions to which short answers can be given, otherwise the exchange may result in a discussion that might not be useful at this stage. Also, early in the course or session, be prepared for limited responses until the group has settled down and individuals feel that they can express their views.

Start involvement with a short introductory or icebreaking activity

Activities that involve the learning group at an early stage in a course or session are particularly useful in letting the participants know how interactive the event is going to be. They have the added advantages of letting the participants start to get to know each other and to move into an interactive, communicating mode. There is a wide range of different types of activities available for a number of different purposes – as described in Chapters 8 and 9 – but at this opening stage activities known as 'introductory' or 'icebreaker' are the most relevant and useful. Another type of activity that is relevant at the start of a course or session is one that requires the learners to solve a problem, perform a negotiation, or undertake some other activity related to the learning topic. In this way the knowledge and skill level of the group can be assessed in a natural and apparently non-testing manner.

Seek expectations

This is an outstandingly useful approach if your opening stage is also the opening session of a more extended course, and serves several purposes. It:

- involves the learners at a very early stage;
- starts to get them used to expressing themselves and their views;
- provides very useful information for the trainer in the rest of the session or course;
- provides a continuity activity that can be repeated at the end of the session or course to help in the assessment of learning satisfaction.

The principal problem related to this activity is the amount of time necessary, not only for the expression of views by the learners, but also the discussion time following the initial stages. However, if time can be built into the training it can be a very valuable training tool.

The participants are given a sheet of flipchart (see Chapter 5 for a description of the uses of flipcharts), prepared as shown in Figure 4.1. On this they are asked to enter their hopes for and needs from the event in one column, and in the other their concerns or fears about it.

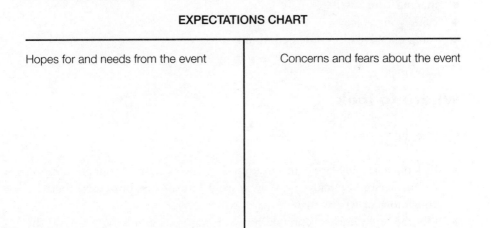

Figure 4.1 An expectations chart

When all the participants have completed their charts these are posted round the walls of the training room and the entries discussed, taking particular note of the concerns and the needs. In addition to considering the time that will be taken by an activity of this nature, consideration must also be given to the extent to which you might be able to do something about the issues that are raised. If you know that issues might be raised about which the learners would expect you to do something but you will not have time, it is safer not to ask the question.

There are a number of different approaches to the start of a course or session that use graphics to help the introductory process (Rae, 2000). Some require more entries than the example used here.

During the presentation or session

It is here that you will be presenting the bulk of your training material. Unless you are going to use a range of activities, etc, it is here that you will be doing the most talking – talking that will need to have an impact. The purpose of this is to get your message across and you will need to use a range of strategies. A number of factors can help you:

- where to look;
- whether to stand or sit;
- how to stand;
- making your case;
- using your voice;
- using effective non-verbal communication;
- having an effective questioning strategy.

Where to look

Use the following:

- Pick out a friendly face in the group and address the start of your presentation to this person. Quickly move away from him or her, however, otherwise your more or less permanent stare will embarrass them.
- Use the 'lighthouse' technique by sweeping your gaze slowly around the group as you talk, switching your eye movements and stopping from time to time to avoid making the technique obvious. Watch for the people at the ends of rows or such seating as 'U' shapes – it is all too easy not to look at them at all, making them feel ignored.

Avoid:

- Staring at individuals, particularly for a longer than normal time. They might start wondering why you are doing this, what you are going to do next, whether you are going to pick on them and so on, and will stop listening actively to what you are saying.
- Looking over the heads of the people all the time, perhaps at the clock at the back of the room. They will notice this and wonder why they are being avoided and whether there is something more interesting going on elsewhere, or are you only interested in the time?

● Rattling keys or coins in your pocket – the audience will start listening to/ for it rather than to what you are saying.

Whether to stand or sit

This decision is often a personal preference, depending on whether either approach makes you feel more comfortable and at ease or is imposed on you by the physical circumstances of the event. If you are working with a small group sitting fairly close to you it is much more effective to sit, but if you are addressing a very large group it is essential for you to stand, otherwise not all the group will see you and you will not see all of them.

How to stand

● Stand as naturally as the circumstance allows you to, without slouching or, men particularly, without a hand in your trouser pocket where you may be tempted to jingle your coins and/or keys.

● If a table has been provided, unless you want to keep the event very formal and non-reactive, move from behind it and stand at its side. You can use the table for your brief and other papers, and these will be readily visible.

● Do not sit on the corner of the table, although this is a natural position, because you may be tempted to swing your legs, a movement that will possibly distract the attention of the group away from listening to you.

● Do not sit on the table in a front, central position because, in addition to encouraging leg movement, it can be seen by the group as a 'power', dominating position, harking back to a typical school classroom with a dominating teacher!

● A lectern is even worse to be behind than a table, as if it is tall it will hide most of you and lessen your contact with the group. Again, a lectern is useful to hold your papers, but stand to one side and move away from it from time to time, for legitimate reasons.

● Do not stand rooted to the spot with no movement, but do not go to the other extreme and prowl around in front of the group all the time you are talking. Movement will be natural and probably sufficient if you have to move over from your main position – where you may have an overhead projector that you are using – to a flipchart or whiteboard, which you will refer to or use.

● If you have something particularly important to say, of which you want the group to take particular notice, move towards them as you speak. Taking a step or two backwards can have the reverse effect or can suggest that you have finished a particular point and want to give them time to consider it.

How to sit

- The adverse effect of sitting behind a table has been commented on and the recommended movement is to the side, even if this means obviously moving the chair to this position. This can give a signal to the group that you want to reduce the formality of the event.
- You may need to sit for some periods of the session, say for example when you are using an overhead projector. When you have finished, stand, and if it is a natural movement, walk over to another training aid you might be using.
- When sitting, relax. If the chair has arms do not clench these so that your knuckles go white – however nervous you may be feeling!
- At one time trainers were recommended to sit with their hands loosely crossed on their lap, except when using them. Do not feel inhibited by this injunction – it can make you appear to be a robot, seated there with your hands crossed and not moving. If you feel you must move your hands, do so; if you want to cross your legs, do so but carefully; move around in the chair when you want to, but don't appear uneasy. Sit reasonably upright, but not ramrod stiff – push your bottom to the back of the chair and you will more naturally sit upright.

Whether you will be expected to, or need to stand or sit, use a table or lectern, and whether it will be possible for you to move about in front of and around the group, will need to be part of your pre-event checks. But when you are with the group do not be bound by any apparent 'rules' – use your common sense, based on how you would like a trainer to behave if you were part of the group.

Making your case

The major part of your session will probably be making your case – imparting the knowledge or information or describing the relevant skills. To do this, following a logical and clear structure is recommended:

- State in summary form your information, view, description, etc.
- Develop your arguments, showing evidence and proof to support them, including counters to opposing arguments that you will have anticipated.
- Repeat, again in summarized form, the arguments you have delivered.
- Unless this has happened during the body of the session, seek questions, views, agreement and so on from the group.

- Review any discussion and summarize the main points.
- Summarize the key points of the session.

Much of this may seem to be solely repetition, but many researchers believe that this is necessary, particularly in complex subjects, to enable learning to take place. Obviously the repetition is not made parrot-fashion, but presented in different words, ways and approaches.

The sequencing of the main body of your material has been discussed earlier – moving from the known to the unknown, simple to the complex, etc. The approach you use will depend on a number of factors, including the information you will have obtained in earlier analyses of the group – what they know already, what their level of understanding is, what level of skill they have – linked with the nature and the complexity of the subject.

The often quoted question 'How do you eat an elephant?' and the answer 'In bite-sized chunks' are relevant in presenting material, especially with complex or extensive data.

Using your voice

However well prepared, interesting or informative your material may be, if you present it in an ineffective manner there is little guarantee that learning will be achieved. How you use your voice can have a significant effect on how you are received, and a useful mnemonic is 'The 4 Ps':

Project your voice, so that the volume is linked to the size of the group and the room, ensuring that everyone can hear without difficulty.

Pronounce your words carefully. Have you a regional accent? If so, how strong is it and could it cause some people problems? Make sure that your word endings are pronounced as clearly as the earlier part of the word, otherwise some of the sense may be lost. Check on the pronunciation of complex or difficult words, or ones that were previously unknown to you. Make sure that you pronounce all the relevant syllables of multi-syllable words – but don't make this sound artificial.

Pause frequently. Doing so gives you time to think about what you are saying and what you will say next, and also gives the listeners time to catch up with the content of your words. Pauses are also very useful for effect – before an important word or statement, for example, thus alerting the listeners to the fact that they should listen to what is coming. Don't be worried by short silences, they will seem longer to you than to the listeners.

Pace variation. A delivery at a constant pace becomes monotonous and is likely to turn off the listeners. Increasing the speed of delivery can impart a feeling of importance or excitement and the listeners can be stimulated to increase their speed of reception. Slow the delivery down and what is said can sound more dramatic and again emphasize importance.

Another mnemonic to help you to remember important aspects of your presentation is 'MERK':

Modulate the tone of your voice to make it interesting – this modulation should be linked with the pace mentioned above. Use drama, apparent monotony, harshness, softness and so on.

Emphasize certain parts of your speaking for effect.

Repeat key words and phrases to emphasize their importance and to ensure understanding and recall.

Keep your eyes away from your notes, only glancing at them when you want to refer to something or remind you of your progress.

Using effective non-verbal communication

Communication and language are not only spoken – what your body says, whether you are speaking or not, says as much, if not more than the words you are speaking. The amount of acceptance of presentations varies, according to research, depending on the situation in which it is given, its complexity, its importance, etc. Your impact as a speaker on the audience is in the ratio represented in Figure 4.2, as described by Professor Albert Mehrabian. This shows that your words have only minimal impact compared with the way you use your voice – which itself has less impact than the visual signals you give out.

These visual factors include your:

- **Facial expression**. Does the way you look agree with the words you are saying and the manner in which you are saying them? For example, what is another person to make of your real feelings if, having asked you for something you say 'Sorry', but do so with a big smile on your face, or say this in a very disinterested tone of voice?
- **Gestures**. There is nothing wrong with moving your hands and arms about while you are speaking, but are you doing this so excessively that the group watches these movements rather than listens to you? 'Stabbing' with the extended finger can often be a useful way of emphasizing a point, but do

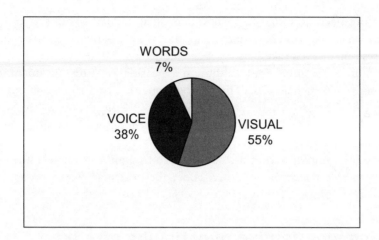

Figure 4.2 Speaker impact

you do this too frequently and towards the same person? This can be interpreted as an attack, the pointed finger changing into a fist!

- **Body language**. In your posture do you insinuate interest or disinterest, a paternal attitude to the group or a demonstration of your power over them? The latter can often be suggested by your sitting astride a chair with the back of the chair facing the group.
- **Eye gaze**. As suggested earlier, where and how you look at the group as you speak can have an effect on their reception of you – do you look at them naturally and with movement, or do you stare at them or past them? If you are asking one person in a group, look at that person; if you are asking the question generally of the group, lighthouse your gaze as you wait for them to respond.
- **Mannerisms**. Everybody has some mannerism, verbal or non-verbal, as they interact with a person or group. What are yours, and are they so many and so pronounced that your listener(s) is too intent on taking notice of them to listen to what you are saying? Have a colleague watch you and give you feedback – you will be surprised at how many you have! Try to moderate them, not get rid of them all, as this will tend to make your interactions unnatural and forced. Only be concerned if they are getting in the way.

One of the most common verbal mannerisms that can interfere with the smooth flow of and listening to a presentation is the number of 'Ums and 'Arrs' that people utter, particularly when they are under some stress, such as when they are new trainers in front of a group. Avoid this habit – such sounds become more noticeable than small natural silences. It has been known for a learning group to count the number of these utterances during a session, or even take bets on their frequency.

Similar common noises, although appearing as words, are unconscious expressions, such as 'OK'. This can be a question or a statement and over-repetition can result in the group responding 'OK' on later occasions. Another can be 'You know', which is an unnecessary interjection at any time!

Non-verbal communication is a substantial and significant subject, the use of which can have a negative or positive effect on a principally verbal presentation, so you are recommended to refer to specialist books on the subject.

Having an effective questioning strategy

One useful technique that a trainer can use in an input session to involve the learners is to ask questions at different stages. These can help to involve them by speaking, can elicit information, can help to determine the level of knowledge or experience of individuals and so on. But beware! Just because you ask a question it does not follow that you will get a response. And a most unnerving moment, for a new trainer particularly, is, having asked a question, being met with silence. This happens to every trainer at some time or other and you must ride out the ensuing silence for a while, perhaps thinking:

- Have I asked a question they can't answer?
- Are they taking time to think of a suitable response?
- Did I ask the question in a way that they could not understand?

One or more of these reasons could apply, so let the silence run for a while; if there is still no response try a different approach.

One of the problems encountered by trainers who are not experienced questioners is getting such a short answer that they have to think of a further question to ask to obtain fuller information. Usually what has been asked is a 'closed question' – these only require the answer 'Yes' or 'No', or a short statement of fact. 'Have you experience of managing people?' is a question that is likely to receive the response 'Yes' or perhaps 'Yes. I have.' If that is the only answer you wanted, fine, but it is more likely that you wanted to be told about that experience. So you then have to ask further questions to obtain this wider information.

One simple way of avoiding this questioning problem is to ask an 'open question' instead. In the case quoted above the revised question could be 'What

experience have you had of managing people?' Such a question would be difficult to answer with a simple 'Yes' or 'No'.

Questioning levels

In addition to the types of questions used effectively or incorrectly – open, closed, multiple, leading, hypothetical and so on – questions can be asked at three, progressive levels:

1. Establishing facts: *'What happened when you did that?'*
2. Eliciting feelings: *'How did you feel about what happened?'*
3. Identifying values: *'What did this mean for you?'*

Use of the feelings and values types of questions has to be handled carefully, the trainer having to assess as far as possible whether the individual or group is ready to allow their feelings to be exposed.

Correct and incorrect answers

Even when questions seeking answers are posed correctly and answered, these answers may be correct, partially correct or incorrect. Whichever, there is usually some relevant action to take.

If the answer is correct, you will need to check that the other learners have understood it or agree with it. It may be necessary to ask:

'Does everybody go along with that?'
'Is there anything anyone would like to add to that?'
'Can anyone give an example?'

If the answer is only partially correct, similar questions to those above can be asked. Emphasize your agreement with the answer so far and perhaps add some further information, or ask a supplementary question to take the response further.

If the answer is incorrect, rather than bluntly saying so, the first question above can be employed. The trainer must also self-question whether the question was badly phrased, or related to material that the group have not yet covered. In the latter case it is dangerous to try that sort of ploy deliberately to force a point.

Some final thoughts on making your points

The points that have been covered so far include:

- opening the session in an effective manner;
- considering whether to stand or sit, how and where;
- using the lighthouse technique in looking at the group;
- making your points in a structured and sequenced way;
- using your voice effectively;
- being aware of and using non-verbal communication;
- using effective questioning techniques.

Some further, final suggestions to help you make your presentations or input sessions effective include:

- Keep the session to the minimum necessary to ensure that the participants learn, rather than receive an overload.
- Always signal your intentions to let the group know what is coming next, particularly when a new topic is going to be raised (or perhaps to wake them up!) by saying:
  - 'What I'd like to do now is. . .'
  - 'What I'd like to discuss with you now is. . .'
  - 'Let's summarize what we have covered so far. . .'
  Or using words clearly and emphatically:
  - 'Significant.'
  - 'Important.'
  - 'The key to the matter is. . .'
- Use examples and analogies, particularly real-life ones. Difficult and complex issues can often be simplified by using an analogy, preferably one with which the audience is familiar.
- Respond to the audience's needs, answering their unspoken question 'What's in it for me?' Most learning groups are at the session to get something out of it for themselves – information, learning, skill, knowledge. So in addition to ensuring that *your* objectives are satisfied, go as far as you can in satisfying *their* objectives. To do this you will obviously need to have some indication of what these are – one method has been suggested, namely the use of the 'Expectations Chart', but a major part of the evaluation of effective learning is knowing where the learners are coming from, where they want to go, where you want them to go, and, at the end, where they have got to.

Hopefully the end result is as much in line as possible with the starting needs and objectives.

- Summarize frequently, but not so frequently as to annoy the learners. This is particularly helpful when the subject matter is complex – summarize at the end of each point and discussion, then make a composite summary at the end.

Finally – and this advice will be detailed in Chapter 6 – illustrate your verbal presentations with as much visual material as possible – graphics, posters, overhead projector slides and so on. You will soon realize that 'a picture is worth a thousand words'.

5

Using Training Aids

I have mentioned several times that talking alone in an input session is not likely to encourage learning, and even, depending on a range of factors, may inhibit it. Your learners are accustomed, in their normal lives, to watching television, which is essentially a mixture of voices and images. You cannot hope to challenge a television programme in your session, but it is valuable to learn the lesson from that source of images, graphics, aids and other supports to the verbal presentation. In training and development these are commonly known as training aids, or sometimes as 'visual aids'. A verbal presentation supported by a balanced selection of some of these aids will help to ensure that you hold the interest of the learners from start to finish and also make a maximum impact on their learning faculties.

Whichever training aids you use some hints are:

- Ensure that they are up to date.
- Ensure that the information on them is correct.
- If they are paper or acetate aids, replace them if they have become dirty, dog-eared or torn.
- If you are not sure how to operate some form of technological aid effectively, do not attempt to use it.
- Wherever possible use images or other forms of graphics rather than words – too many training aids simply repeat the words you are using.

The most common training aids in use include:

a particular object;	the presenter;
flipcharts or posters;	whiteboards;
overhead projectors (OHPs);	audio equipment;
audio-visual equipment;	video and video triggers.
handouts;	

In this chapter we will consider the first five above. Audio equipment, etc, is discussed in Chapter 6.

A particular object

Where relevant, the most effective training aid is to have the actual object under discussion physically present. In such cases the object requires little verbal description – objects speak for themselves, although obviously in a training environment descriptions of the component parts, their operation and their use will form the commentary. Training events in which this type of aid is usually used are workshop or desk training, and it is here that the technique 'Tell, show, do' is particularly apt.

For example, if the training event concerned the computer there would be one available for the trainer to use, with, preferably, individual computers for each participant linked to the trainer's master. The trainer would 'Tell' the group about the use of the computer and describe its components. The actual computer would then be used in a 'Showing' phase, in which the trainer would: a) show the components on the computer, and b) demonstrate the particular aspects of its use. In the final 'Do' phase the learners would be let loose on their computers to try out what they had been told about and shown. In a complex issue such as this the session would be broken down into sections, each following the 'Tell, show, do' technique.

It will not always be possible to have the object itself in the training room. In such cases it may be possible to take the group on a 'field trip' to see it *in situ*, for example when the training concerns a giant earth remover. Otherwise the event would have to be limited to the use of a photograph, a small object that can be passed around, or a model (preferably a working one).

The presenter

Although many presenters of training sessions do not appreciate the fact, they are themselves one of the most powerful and visible training aids, and can have considerable impact on the learning group. For example, if the session subject is motivation, in which enthusiasm and commitment are included as aspects of this behaviour, the learners are less likely to take notice if the trainer before them does not exhibit these behaviours. A typical example of the deliberate use of the person as the training aid is seen at the start of every flight, when the cabin staff demonstrate on *themselves* the use of the lifesaving equipment.

Appearance and dress can have a strong influence on the attitudes of the group towards the trainer, although under normal circumstances these are not considered as aids. There are a number of circumstances when they can become so, however; for example during an induction programme when the objective is to show new employees the appearance and dress acceptable in the organization's culture, or perhaps to initiate a discussion on a proposed new dress code (or cessation of one), on a new form of 'uniform', and so on.

The flipchart

The flipchart is one of the most frequently used aids on training and development courses. It is basically a pad of fairly strong A1 size paper, mounted on an easel by either ring holes and pegs, or by a strong spring-hinged clip. It is one of the modern equivalents of the old black- or greenboard, with marker pens replacing messy chalk.

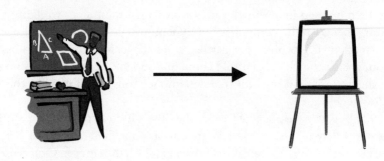

Figure 5.1 The flipchart

Advantages

- **Adaptable.** Can be used with either a blank sheet on which to write or draw to start, or as a prepared sheet or poster, the parts being disclosed in a variety of ways.
- **Any paper usable.** Although heavyweight flipchart paper is commercially available and is commonly used, any large sheet of paper is suitable.
- **Easy to use.** Few basic skills, other than clear and effective writing in large print or script.
- **No power requirement.** Unlike more sophisticated, electric/electronic aid equipment, no power supply is required so it can be used anywhere.

- **Easily displayed.** Sheets of paper, even the A1 size of the usual flipchart, are relatively light and can be posted on the easel, walls, doors, cabinets and even curtains using a dry, reusable material such as Blu-Tack.
- **Retainable for reference.** Unlike the blackboard, from which the writing has to be erased for reuse, each used sheet of flipchart can be removed from the easel and retained for later reference or other use.
- **Simple, cheap, needs little training.** A principal advantage for new trainers. The necessary training is in how to write legibly on a vertical-standing sheet of paper, maintaining level lines, and also the use of techniques to introduce impact.
- **Transportable.** The sheets of paper can be easily rolled up and the stand collapsed for transportation. Smaller than A1 stands or flipchart display folders are available that are even easier to carry, although their use in a group can be more limited.
- **Ready for immediate recording.** No prior preparation is necessary if the flipchart is to be used as a large 'jotting' pad during a session.

Disadvantages

- **Easily torn, dirtied and dog-eared.** Although easily portable, the sheets can be difficult to store and transport safely as they are also easily damaged.
- **Can look unprofessional.** If badly prepared they can lose their impact on the learning group and reduce the trainer's credibility.
- **Special techniques difficult.** The commonly used techniques of covering pre-prepared entries with cards held by paper clips or Blu-Tack can cause problems. Constant reference backwards and forwards can be aided by the use of clips or folds, but without care these techniques can go wrong.
- **Usually only of a temporary value.** Because paper is used, this aid has only a limited life, which can reduce its value if the material is sufficiently important to be retained and reused.

Flipchart presentation tips

The flipchart can be an extremely useful aid during a training session and, although it can be used in a very straightforward, simple manner, there are additional ways to enhance its use.

Invisible writing

If you are unsure how much space will be used on a flipchart during the session, are not used to writing freehand on flipcharts, are frightened that your writing

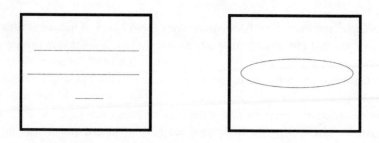

Figure 5.2 Outline traces

will slide away from the horizontal (a very common occurrence), or are not sure about drawing a graphic in front of the group, you can prepare a faint outline prior to the session.

The dotted outlines in Figure 5.2 represent faint pencil lines or outlines along which text can be written as it becomes relevant or the graphic filled in. If the lines are fairly faint, but dark enough to be seen by the trainer standing at the flipchart, they will not be seen by the group at a distance.

Brief corner crib

There will be times when you have to move away from your brief to the flipchart (or other aid) and may be concerned that you will forget what you have to enter on the chart. In the top right corner of the chart, lightly pencil in so that you (but not the group) can see key words of the material you are to enter. You will then not have to carry your brief with you when you leave your main position.

Bookmarking

There may be times when you are using a flipchart that, having completed some sheets, you wish to refer to one or two of them later in the session. Some trainers fold a bottom corner to identify these, but I find that my folds inexplicably disappear. Instead, slip paper clips on to the bottom of the specific sheets. To be really clever use one, two or more clips depending on the order in which you will want to refer to them.

You can 'bookmark' prepared sheets in a similar way if you know you will, at some stage, want to refer to a sheet later in the pack. Folds or paper clips may not be 'safe', so in this case, rather than refer to a sheet later in the pack, have a duplicate ready at the stage you want to use it.

Tearing sheets from the pack

Some pads of flipchart sheets have a line of perforations near the top of the sheets to facilitate tearing them off, but if you do not have these be careful how you do it – it is all too easy to tear off a jagged piece or even tear the sheet in two. Try scoring lightly across the sheet with a craft knife and tearing the first half-inch or so before the session.

Finishing with an aid

When you have finished using a flipchart sheet, as with any other training aid, get rid of it. Either detach the sheet and fix it to the training room wall, flip it over the top of the stand, or tear it off and waste it. Leaving the chart on view encourages the participants to keep looking at it rather than giving you their full attention.

Colours, sizes and graphics

Even if your favourite colours tend towards the pastel shades and light yellows, reds and greens, avoid them. The lighting, whether artificial or natural (bright sun, for example) can make them very difficult, if not impossible, to see.

Write more clearly and larger than you would normally do or think of doing. Small, slightly unclear writing may appear obvious to you standing beside the flipchart, but to a learner seated some distance away it may mean nothing. Write more slowly than you are accustomed to – this will help you form the letters more effectively.

Draw plenty of images or graphics on your flipcharts to support or replace your words. If you can't draw, pre-prepared flipcharts can be illustrated with pictures taken from journals or magazines – make sure they are large enough to be seen and identified from a distance. If you have an epivisor or epidiascope (a projector that projects an image of a solid object – eg a sheet of paper or even a three-dimensional object – on to a screen) project your illustration on to the flipchart and copy as much as you can of the image to whatever size you require.

Lettering appearance

There have been several anecdotal accounts or reported research on the use of particular types of lettering to improve clarity. Publishers of books and journals principally use a serif type of script (eg Times), suggesting that it is clearer to read and easier on the readers' eyes – this may be purely tradition. Most trainers for their handouts, flipchart and OHP slides use sans serif (eg Arial), claiming that it is easier to read – perhaps because it is also easier to write than with serif. Much of this may fall to personal preference – I prefer to use sans serif for any writing I do, of whatever nature; this again may simply be habit. The crux is whether the group can read your visual aid. A well-presented chart, attractive, clear, uncluttered and not looking like a rainbow will have impact and will serve its purpose.

Additive and disclosure techniques

The most common method of using the flipchart, which utilizes the methods described above, is known as the additive technique, when you start with a blank flipchart and add writing or drawing to it during the session.

A reverse method is the disclosure system, when the flipchart has been pre-prepared, but is so constructed that:

- Not all the chart is visible at once.
- The items on the chart can be disclosed one at a time.
- The order of disclosure is flexible.

A pre-prepared flipchart will normally show a list of words or phrases or perhaps the stages of a process that will be discussed during a session. If the whole chart is displayed while you were speaking about, say, item two, the group will read on and may have reached item six, possibly having missed a lot of what you were saying and also not necessarily understanding the stages to come.

There are two main techniques for dealing with this. First, if there are only two or three items on the chart the sheet can be folded to hide those following the first. As each entry is to be discussed it can be disclosed by unfolding the relevant fold, the folds being held by Blu-Tack or paper clips. The principal disadvantage invokes 'Murphy's Law' as at inopportune times the folds can come undone.

The second technique is certainly easier to use and looks more professional. When there are more than two or three entries or folding does not appear appropriate, disclosure masks can be made. These are rectangular pieces of paper, or preferably card, cut sufficiently large to cover each entry individually. They can be held to the chart by Blu-Tack or, if they extend to the edges of the chart, by paper clips. When the session reaches the entry to be discussed it is 'disclosed' by the simple expedient of removing the relevant mask.

Advantages of the disclosure technique

- The group cannot read in advance items that you have not reached.
- You are not restricted to disclosing the items in order, as you would be with the folds, selecting the entries according to the way in which you have run that part of the session on this occasion.

Disadvantages of the disclosure technique

Two disadvantages to the disclosure technique are apparent, 'apparent' because only one is a real disadvantage.

The apparent one is that the entries in the chart are covered by the masks, and unless you can remember what is underneath you may disclose the wrong item. This can be simply remedied by using the ubiquitous faint pencil. On the mask write an indication of what is underneath. Again, you will be able to see this crib but the learning group will not.

The real problem when you have a chart with a number of entries covered is that some of the learning group may engage in a silent guessing game of what is hidden, and also, as you disclose some items, they start counting how many are left! These might contribute to non-listening, but unfortunately there is nothing you can do to avoid this other than ensure somehow that they listen actively and take part in the session by question and answer, discussion and so on.

Talking and writing

One of the principal problems encountered by newcomers to the flipchart in front of an audience is when to talk and when to write. A strongly recommended method, in order to stop your lines flowing down to the right, is to stand facing the flipchart when writing. If you do this while you are talking, however:

● you will be talking to the flipchart, not the group, and your valuable message may be lost;
● you have lost contact with the group for the time you are turned away from them.

So when you have to write on the flipchart stop talking, turn to the flipchart and write as quickly but as clearly as you can. The silence will seem interminable to you, but in fact will not be as long as it seems and the audience will not be disturbed unless you do take a very long time. When you have finished writing stand away from the flipchart to let the audience see what you have written. You will need to take these pauses into account when you are timing your presentation.

Miscellaneous guidelines for the use of the flipchart

● Before you start the session ensure that there is sufficient paper on the flipchart pad, that the same applies to flipcharts in syndicate rooms, and that you have spare flipcharts readily available.
● Check that all markers are of the correct type, you have the required colours, and that they all work.

- Ensure that the easel/stand is stable and upright.
- When you pre-prepare a number of flipchart sheets leave a blank sheet after each prepared one so that you do not immediately flip to the next chart – you may not be ready for it. This will also ensure that the first sheet does not ink through to a sheet that has been prepared.

The whiteboard

As the flipchart was a development of the blackboard, so the whiteboard is from the flipchart. It consists of a metal sheet, coated with white plastic (although different coloured surfaces are available), usually gloss-finished, and mounted to the front wall of a training room. In larger training rooms these whiteboards can also be found in additional locations around the room. Whiteboards are usually large, ranging from about 2–3 m × 1–2 m, although it is possible to obtain smaller, portable ones down to about 15 cm × 10 cm, and ones in the middle range, up to about A1 size, that can be mounted on easel stands like the traditional flipchart.

The whiteboard is mostly used like the flipchart, but is written on with special dry marker pens that can be easily erased with a duster. One major problem that can arise is when inexperienced people use the wrong type of pens and erasure has to done with special cleaning fluid.

The whiteboard, then, is not usually as transportable as the flipchart, but with the size of the board entries can be made on it wherever is suitable. In addition to using the correct dry marker pens care has to be taken against accidentally erasing or smudging what has been written. I have suffered at the hands of enthusiastic cleaning staff who had 'helped' me in the evening by cleaning the whiteboard – unfortunately I had wanted the entries for training the following day! Leave a large note attached to or written on the board to avoid this!

Colours and drawn graphics are used for impact on the whiteboard in very much the same way as on the flipchart. As suggested above, there are dangers in preparing too much in advance, and of course once the entries have been erased they have gone permanently. But during a session, as a 'notepad' to record comments, ideas, stages and so on that can be erased to enable the entry of more material, it has no equal. Because the metal sheet from which it is constructed is usually magnetic pictures with small magnets attached can be used in addition to pens, thus extending the creative possibilities. It can also be used as a screen, preferably when the surface is matt, for an OHP or other projector, but because of its usual vertical fixing in one position projection and sighting problems can occur.

More recently electronic whiteboards have been produced, usually with three or more flexible whiteboards in a continuous strip that can be moved round to present a new writing surface without erasing material already entered. Some of these e-whiteboards have the additional capability of producing paper-printed A4 copies of the material written on one of the panes – useful when an immediate handout is required.

Advantages

The advantages of the whiteboard include many of those described for the flipchart. The main ones are:

- simple to use;
- entries can be erased and re-entered very easily;
- no power required, except in the case of the e-whiteboards;
- can use magnetic holders;
- versatile;
- cleaner than chalkboard;
- ease of use, apart from writing on an unaccustomed surface.

Disadvantages

- Facing away from group.
- Less easy to use as permanent poster.
- Special markers needed.
- Writing difficulties on a large, shiny surface.
- Unprofessional looking when writing is messy and material is scrawled all over the board. (It is easier to look on a large whiteboard as a series of A1 flipcharts and keep within a rough area until one of these is full.
- Easily erased – too easily.)
- Special effects not easy – the whiteboard is designed for (and constrained by) writing and drawing and, in most modern cases, magnetic effects. Unless the last of these are used, disclosure is not as simple as in the case of the flipchart, and even with the electronic whiteboard 'flipped sheets' are restricted to the number of sheet panels contained therein.
- Power-cut problems with electronic versions.

The overhead projector

Close behind the flipchart and whiteboard in popularity and availability is the overhead projector, universally abbreviated to OHP. It projects images, usually from acetate squares or other transparent film, on to a screen. As shown in Figure 5.3, it consists of a box, A, that contains a light source, projecting light upwards through a semi-opaque glass screen known as a Fresnel lens, B; the light concentrating on the OHP head, C. In the movable head are a further lens and a reflecting mirror, D. The image on the transparency slide that is placed on the Fresnel lens is projected on to a screen, usually about 1.5 m square and some 4 m or so away from the OHP. Fitted on the light-box are an on/off switch, a switch or lever to reduce refraction discolouring, and (on some models) a switch to move between the main projection bulb and a spare in case the original one burns out. The image is focused by a small wheel fitted to the head that can move up and down the headpost, E.

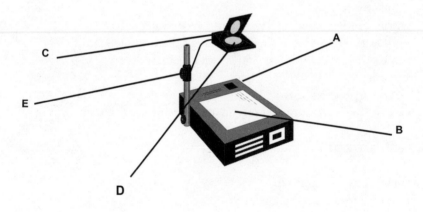

Figure 5.3 The standard OHP

There is a wide range in the quality of OHPs, the differences being the quality of materials used, the features fitted, the interchangeability of the focusing lens for enlarged or reduced projected images, silent-running fans or other means of heat dispersion, the availability of projector bulb switching and the quality of the bulb itself. Some OHPs are fitted to be linked with computers and others to large projection equipment; another variety is a portable model that is much smaller and lighter than the standard model.

The OHP is one of the most flexible training aids generally available and can be very useful in learning because of the range it offers in support of the trainer's approach and the participants' learning. The images to be projected can be written and drawn on:

- acetate squares that can be framed if required;
- other transparent films used in the same way;
- continuous rolls of acetate film that can be wound over and past the Fresnel Lens; and even
- small solid objects can be placed on the OHP for silhouette projection.

Advantages

- Wide availability.
- Portability.
- Group visual contact – the trainer is facing the audience even when using the projector.
- Used from a standing or sitting position.
- High visual impact – a large, bright and impactive image can be produced and the image is visible even in broad daylight.
- Scalable image – large images are as easily produced as small ones, the size being determined by the screen on to which the image is thrown, or the size of the group/training room.
- Relatively cheap.
- Small object projection – small solid objects can be placed on the Fresnel Lens and projected as two-dimensional silhouettes.
- Transparencies, whether framed or unframed, are easily portable even in substantial numbers.
- Easy transparency production – the transparencies or slides can be produced on the acetate squares with permanent or erasable marker pens, dry lettering, computer programs, by professional producers and so on.
- Flexibility of use – all the techniques described for the flipchart and the whiteboard are possible with the OHP, usually in a more effective form. OHP transparencies can either be pre-prepared or produced during an event, in the same way that we saw with flipchart posters and whiteboard entries. A variety of techniques also can be employed, principally the additive and disclosure techniques, although the latter can have a wider range of variations than is possible with the flipchart.

Disadvantages

- Needs electricity – this is a problem only in times of power cuts. However, if these are a common at the time of the session a back-up set of prepared flipcharts is advisable.
- Needs a screen – the image is best presented on the correct type of screen, but can be projected on to almost any light-coloured, flat surface.
- Annoying illumination – unless you are showing a number of slides in rapid succession it is advisable to switch off between projections, as a large bright, blank area can be very distracting. However, if a number of slides are being used close together a switch on/switch off in between each can be most annoying to the viewing group.
- Obscuring – you will need to be careful that the vertical post holding the projection mirror does not obscure part of the screen.
- Noise – older OHPs had a very noisy fan, but later and more expensive models have a different method of heat dispersion.
- Bulb burnout – this is not unknown in the middle of a session! Most modern OHPs have a reserve bulb that can be brought into operation by means of a switch. If not, it is a wise precaution to have a spare bulb in your trainer's toolkit.
- Overcrowding – because it is easy to make entries on an acetate sheet there is a temptation to crowd on masses of information, so losing the impact of an effective slide.

Keystoning

Keystoning is an effect that occurs with the use of an OHP – it is sometimes avoidable, sometimes not. It can be avoided by setting up the projector and screen in a compatible conjunction. The following guidance should help in achieving this:

1. Place the OHP on a table so that the head is about 1 m above the floor. You will need to be prepared to adapt this height in view of any problems you may encounter later.
2. Ensure that all lenses and mirrors are clean. You will be surprised by the effect of dust particles or smears, many times enlarged, when projected on to the screen.
3. Set up the screen. The optimum position for this will depend on the size and shape of the training room, and the size and positioning of the group, but in general it is usually best erected across the front left corner of the room, behind and to the right of the trainer or presenter. This will also

help to obtain the largest image feasible. Figure 5.4 demonstrates this positioning – the OHP will have to be placed similarly, at an angle facing the screen. This angling in fact helps to make both the OHP screen and the trainer as visible as possible – both desirable attributes from the learning point of view.

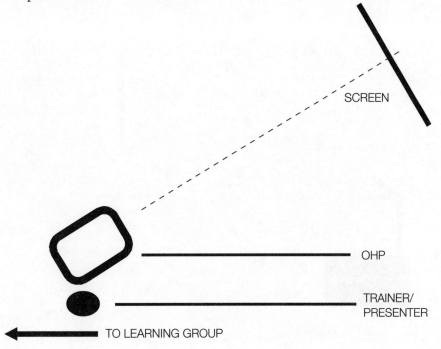

Figure 5.4 Positioning the OHP and screen

The keystoning effect happens when the OHP and screen are set up incorrectly and the projected image has a distorted shape, as shown in Figure 5.5.

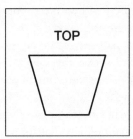

Figure 5.5 Keystoning

Keystoning is produced by the light beam from the OHP not being at an angle of 90 degrees to the screen. The more the deviation from this angle the greater the keystoning effect. This is shown in Figure 5.6, the deviation of the light beam from the 90-degree angle being very obvious.

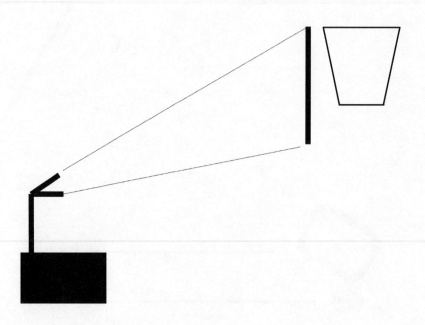

Figure 5.6 OHP positioning causing keystoning

Keystoning can be avoided, or minimized, by using the extending arm at the top of the column of most screens. This arm swings out forwards and the screen can be attached to this so that it is tilted forward. If necessary the OHP itself can be tilted and with this combination keystoning can be avoided altogether. Care must be taken if the OHP is tilted, however, that this is not done so as to jeopardize the safety of the OHP and the slides placed upon it. Figure 5.7 shows this effect.

4. Ensure that the screen can be seen from all parts of the room. Raising the screen to maximum height (watch out for keystoning) and moving the screen away from the corner position can help improve visibility.

There are two principal culprits that interrupt the group's view of the screen – the trainer sitting beside the OHP and the headpost of the OHP. Both might be avoided by moving the OHP slightly, and by lowering the

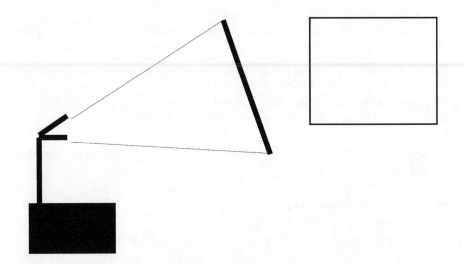

Figure 5.7 Keystoning avoided by tilting screen

headpost (again watch out for keystoning). It will be necessary to experiment with different positions of the OHP, screen and trainer to achieve maximum visibility, each move being checked by a colleague trying out the seats where the group will sit. You can yourself check visibility problems caused by the screen and the OHP, but obviously not your own position beside the equipment. In an extreme situation, I have solved this last problem by using a pile of books on the seat beside the OHP!

5. The OHP can produce disturbing colour fringes with the screen image, usually blue or red. These can usually be eliminated by means of a lever attached to the light-box. If there is not one fitted – as in the case of cheaper, basic OHPs – you may have to readjust the tilt of the OHP and/or screen: back to the problem of keystoning!

6. Ensure that the image is in focus by testing with a typical transparency, and again check this from different parts of the room.

7. Check the projection bulb again and also the spare bulb switching facility, if one is fitted; otherwise check that you have your own spare and know how to fit it.

The production of effective slides or transparencies for the OHP is an art (and a science) in itself, requiring more space than is available here; but see *Using Training Aids in Training and Development* (Rae, 1998) for substantial advice and guidance on this topic.

The following is a summary of advice on using this very useful training aid.

- Use relevant-sized lettering.
- Up to 15 m, lettering more than 5 mm in height.
- 15–20 m, lettering more than 10 mm in height.
- Above 20 m, lettering no less than 15 mm in height.
- Mix both upper- and lower-case lettering.
- Use clearest form of lettering available – freehand, dry lettering, computer generated.
- Never use typescript.
- Leave plenty of space between lines.
- Keep the slide uncluttered.
- Aim for maximum of 10 lines per slide – but don't be a slave to this.
- Aim for maximum of six or seven words per line – again don't be a slave.
- Use frames for impact.
- Use colours freely – preferably dark ones.
- Try white letters on a black background.
- Always have a heading for your slide.
- Use graphics, symbols, speech marks and cartoons as often as possible – speech bubbles are particularly useful and impactive.
- The contents – KISS (Keep it short and simple).
- Check OHP is correctly focused and that the bulb works, before the session – and check spare.
- Avoid keystoning.
- Use the various transparency preparation methods available.
- Ensure visibility of the whole screen from all parts.
- Decide whether to sit or stand.
- Watch your talking and writing.

6

Other Training Aids

In Chapter 5 we considered what are probably the most commonly used training aids – the flipchart, the whiteboard and the overhead projector. But there are other aids – some simple, some complex, some traditional, some technological – all of which can enhance the training input session or course. In this chapter we cover:

- handouts;
- audio equipment;
- audio-visual presentations;
- videos and trigger videos;
- computers.

Handouts

Handouts are part of course documentation or training material and are not normally thought of when training aids are being considered, but they are probably one of the most common. Two of the problems of learning are retention and recall. If handouts can be produced so that the learner uses them as references on a continuous and frequent basis these problems will be lessened.

Using handouts

Handouts as training aids have a number of uses and formats, times and methods of use, which include:

- before the event as preparation aids;
- during the event as pre-session support;

- during the event to summarize the training to that point;
- during the event as an interactive instrument;
- briefing notes for activities;
- post-event reminders.

Before the event as preparation aids

Some form of documentation can be issued before the event to prepare the learners for the more detailed or in-depth live sessions. The handout can summarize the areas of learning, recommend pre-event reading and perhaps ask participants to carry out some exercises or projects before the event (such as identifying specific services and practices in their organization, keeping a time diary, obtaining the views of managers in the organization). If all the participants start the training at more or less the same level of knowledge this obviously makes the learning process easier for both them and the trainer.

You must not, however, make assumptions about this pre-event handout. First, there is no guarantee that everybody will read it or act on it. In fact you can be almost certain that somebody will arrive for the event having failed to take any action at all. Four specific actions resulting from this are suggested:

- Accept it and adjust your programme to accommodate the ones who are involved. If the pre-reading was essential you may not be able to avoid this.
- Ignore the fact that essential reading has not been done by one or more participants and carry on as if there was no problem – because of the time allowed for the training you may be forced into this position in spite of the learning problems it may produce.
- Send the non-performers to a separate part of the training location to catch up with the necessary learning – or as far as it is possible at that stage. (Note that this may cause further problems when they return to the event, which will have been progressing in their absence.)
- A draconian action, but practised by at least one organization of which I am aware, is to send the non-compliers (if the failure could have been avoided) back to their organization(s). If the pre-work is absolutely essential to the effectiveness of the learning – the event may be very constrained and need to start from a particular point – have you any real alternative?

If there are so many potential problems, why invite them by sending out pre-event material? Unless it is completely new material for the learners (when they would all be expected to be at the same zero level), most courses, unless there has been some pre-selection, will start with participants at different levels of knowledge and skills. This does not make the task of training and learning any easier, and has been the cause of many of the bad evaluations of training programmes – thus bad evaluations are not necessarily due to the trainers or the training.

During the event as a preparation

Some trainers prefer to issue handouts related to their session(s) at the start on the basis that this will let the learners know what the session is about and what they should be looking for. This handout can be brief or extended. If the latter there are dangers that it will not be used or, worse, will be read as the session progresses, the learners either checking on the trainer or not listening to the presentation.

A much more effective approach is to make this handout very brief, stating only the key points of the session subjects, supporting the verbal, summary statement with which the trainer will (should) start the session.

During the event to summarize the training to that point

One of the principal problems with handouts is ensuring that they are read, which is essential if they are to act as a supportive training aid for the session or event. A successful approach to this problem (although it will eat into the practical time of the event) is to issue the relevant handout at the end of a session or at the end of the sections of a session, *and give the learners time to read it.* The latter is an essential activity and can, if time allows, be developed by discussion or questions on the handout, activity that really should have occurred during the session. As with all handouts, and perhaps even more so in this case, you should ensure that the material accurately reflects the content of the session. There is no argument against including *more* than is mentioned in the session, but you must ensure that the learner is made aware that this was not included in the oral part.

During the event as an interactive instrument

Questions and answers as a result of issuing the handout are included here. The more interactive the use of a handout during the event, the less passive the session. Another example might be at the end of a section of the session (or at the end of the session) when a handout is issued that would ask the learners to *do* something, even if this is merely reflecting on what has happened. Questions might include:

- What happened from their point of view during the activity?
- What activities contributed to this?
- Who was significantly involved during the process?
- What have they learnt from the experience?
- How might they implement the information?
- What problems might arise from the suggested actions?

A final part of such an interactive handout might be combined with a summary of the learning points, the key areas covered, ideas for implementation and so on, this part to be read after the interactive part.

Briefing notes for activities

These are probably the handouts with the greatest use during a session, as learners should follow them when asked to take part in some form of activity. Such handouts should supplement the verbal instructions you will be giving before handing them out and will describe:

- what the activity is;
- what is required as a result of the activity;
- how long the learners have to complete it;
- how they will be required to report their results;
- any comments about equipment or other resources.

This kind of handout should contain sufficient material to enable the learners to carry out the activity. But it should not be too long or too complex to be read and understood. This latter point will have to be carefully considered, however, as the purpose of the activity may indeed be to test the acuity of the learners. Keep the handout brief, with short but understandable sentences; use plenty of 'white space'; and use bullet points and other typographical methods as suggested earlier for visual aids. If at all possible, but not at the expense of clarity, keep the brief to one side of a sheet of A4 paper – if you fill this, redraft the brief as, in many cases, it will be too long.

Above all, give the participants, and observers (who will have their own documents as well as observation instruments with which to familarize themselves), sufficient time to read the brief, understand it and remember the key points. Check this almost to the point of annoyance, because on so many occasions groups of learners have blamed the cause of their 'failure' in the activity on having insufficient time to read and learn the brief.

Post-event reminders

These are documents issued either at the end of each session or at the end of a course, with the intention that they are taken away by the participants as post-event references and recall supports. The obvious hope of the issuers is that the learners will actually use these, reading and rereading them and perhaps using them in their implementation of the learning. However, these hopes are not always (often?) fulfilled and the use of post-event reminders varies considerably. Typical comments by learners about their non-use range from:

- 'I threw them away before I even left the training room',
- 'When I got back to work, I put them in a drawer and never looked at them again',

through

- 'I look at them occasionally to remind me of the content of the presentation',

to

- 'I frequently refer them to remind me of the material and motivate me to practise the learning',
- 'I refer to them when I am constructing a presentation or negotiation of my own',
- 'I use them as handouts at my own events!'.

The negative reasons can range from participants' thinking the handouts badly written to considering that they contain irrelevant or incorrect material. But the principal reason is that they are usually written in such a form as not to invite reading. Check by considering whether *you* would want to read it yourself.

Guidelines for writing handouts

Although these guidelines do not guarantee that your handouts will be read or used, they may increase that likelihood:

- Use no more than two sides of one sheet of A4 wherever possible.
- Reread and edit the handout severely, particularly if it covers more than one or two sides.
- Is another format more effective?
- Use plenty of 'white space'.
- Use copied OHP slides.
- Use bullet lists for impact.
- Use a variety of typo forms – is a serif font or a sans serif font clearer and more easily read?
- Let the learners know at the start of the session whether there will be a handout(s) and what it will or will not cover.
- Wherever possible use graphics instead of words.

Colour and tinting

Most of your handouts and other written material that are produced 'in-house' will be in monochrome, rather than those from professional printing houses where colours can be included (at a cost). However, colour shades can be indicated in monochrome by using a percentage of the shades of black. Most computer programs contain a grey-scale line colour and style and a fill range of shading. This commonly runs from solid black (100 per cent), through varying percentages that appear as progressive depths of grey to clear (0 per cent). These shade fills can be used to modify images, photographs and drawings.

Paper

The paper you use for your handouts or other written material offers significant choices. The range of choices includes:

- colour;
- grain;
- size;
- paper:
  - types;
  - weight.

Colour. A wide variety and range of colours and shades are available and can be very useful in providing an immediate identification code. For example, handouts can be printed on white paper, activity briefs on yellow, and so on. Be careful, however, as an indiscriminate use of lots of colours can be annoying.

Grain. This may not have too much impact on emphasis or appearance, but some papers benefit from an obvious grain running vertically, horizontally or diagonally, and some have a better appearance without any obvious grain. Heavily grained paper can have an effect on the printing quality and it is certainly more difficult to write with a pen on this type of paper.

Size. Although A4 and A5 sizes are the most commonly used paper sizes, there is a range of sizes from large to small, each having a relevance for particular purposes. Paper sizes are described under ISO (International Standards Organization) with A0 as the largest trimmed sheet size of 1 sq m. The sizes reduce, by halving the preceding size, to A10 which is 26 × 37 mm, intermediate sizes including A4 (half of A3) at 210 × 297 mm and A5 (half of A4) at 148 × 210 mm. A4 is the most commonly used size for handouts since a substantial amount of text and graphics can be included on one page, which is a suitable size to be fitted into a ringbinder.

Paper types. There are many types of paper, some of the names given being unique to the manufacturer, although common ones are 'cartridge', which is a heavy and tough paper that is almost card; 'bond', a crisp, tough paper with a matt surface; 'wove', smooth, usually brilliant white with a slightly glossy surface; and 'art', which is very smooth and glossy.

Weight. This factor determines the 'thickness' of the paper and is measured in grammes per square metre and shown by the abbreviation 'gsm' or 'g/m^2'. The minimum weight generally used is 90 gsm, which is the lowest weight of paper that can be printed on both sides without the printing showing through – although the type of paper can also affect this. If you want to print on both sides, your safest weight is 100 gsm.

Handout style

This subject can be one of the most controversial in the area of guidelines for handouts. The 'normal' versus 'white space' format has been mentioned above; this is but one of the areas of possible controversy, the former being favoured usually by people who are not confident that their session was sufficient to enable learning. But other issues can be equally controversial and in many cases evolve into purely personal preference – but is it *your* preference or that of the *learners*?

Consistency

Two principal schools of thought exist in relation to the consistency of handouts – as indeed in many other forms of training aid. Probably the major supporters of the consistency party are book publishers, which, in general, demand that like items are treated in a similar manner. They disapprove, to a large extent, of the mixing of typefaces, size of illustrations and so on, whereas the other camp considers variety makes for a greater degree of interest and impact.

Consistency is almost certainly required within one document. I do not mean by this that there can be no mixing at all, but you should make consistent those aspects that, if mixed, would confuse. If, for example, you always use ■ bullets for major items and ● bullets for sub-items, do so throughout the document. It can be confusing to the reader if your stage lists are numbered 1), 2), etc in one part, and a), b), etc in other parts. This does not, however, necessarily mean that the next document has to follow slavishly the conventions you have formulated for the first: a change of appearance can often improve impact, leading the reader away from 'Oh, here's the same sort of boring handout'.

If you are going to use, for example, personalized or rare symbols in a range of documents it can be helpful to the readers if you include somewhere, perhaps in a first brief handout, an explanation of what these deviations from the norm are.

Use abbreviations sparingly. You may know what they are, but not every reader may. A useful technique is to spell out in full the word or phrase the first time it is used. After this first use the convention is to include the abbreviation in brackets – eg National Vocational Qualification (NVQ) – and I have always found, when reading, that it is helpful if the abbreviation is then used throughout. However, if the abbreviation is not used regularly, later occasions benefit from a repeat of the full phrase.

Be careful of your grammar and spelling; be consistent. For example, if the writing style uses *z* rather than *s* in certain words – organization, formalize, etc – use the z consistently.

Graphs, tables and charts in handouts

If figures or text are printed in a reasonable size any form of table or chart can be used. But the criterion is, still, keep them as clear and as simple as possible. A large, complicated table will not encourage examination and its value will be lost. Obviously there will be occasions when simplicity in a table will not be possible: this may be the occasion to consider another form of presentation.

The principal presentation formats utilizing numerical data in use for handouts include:

● tables;
● pie charts;
● bar and column charts;
● line graphs;
● decision or logical trees.

All these are available in simple computer software programs and are easy to construct (many of the formats with several variations) and can enhance and clarify almost any handout.

Audio equipment

In training sessions 'audio equipment' generally refers to cassette players and associated equipment, which have a useful, albeit limited use in presentations. The video attracts much more interest with its combination of sound and movement, and its familiarity to the viewers as part of everyday life.

But in a training session the playing of a short excerpt from a cassette, produced either by the presenter or, more usually, some expert in the subject, can change the atmosphere and pace of the session, affording the audience a break from the presenter and vice versa! Sometimes part of the presentation is complex and the use of exact wording is essential – the pre-recorded audio cassette can be used for this purpose very effectively and accurately.

Apart from direct support to the training, it can be used as background music while the participants are assembling, a time when both the presenter and the audience may be feeling a little strange and strained, or perhaps, quietly, when the groups are working on a practical project. Some practitioners believe that music can have a very positive effect in the learning process (Millbower, 2000).

An alternative presentational use for the audio cassette, borrowed from training and self-development activities, is for it to be listened to when driving. Played on a personal cassette player, it can also be listened to at home or while travelling by rail or air.

Audio-visual presentations

Cassettes can be combined in one projector with 35mm slides as a table-top projector for small groups. The projector projects either manually or automatically a programme of 35mm slides to the accompaniment of a verbal presentation on cassette that can be electronically synchronized with the slides. The size of the group can be increased, as many of these combination player-projectors can also be simply converted to project the image on to a large screen.

Care must be taken that the slides are all properly mounted and inserted in the projector carriage, otherwise problems might occur with jamming. Once started you have only little control over the process, other than stopping and restarting the programme. Returning to a subject as the result of, say, a question from a member of the group can be extremely difficult and the programme, once established, is confined to that material. Custom-made, self-produced programmes that run automatically or semi-automatically are quite simple to produce if you have the required electronic pulse equipment.

Videos

Videos, both 'home-made' and professionally produced, have taken over from film, and themselves are in the process of being taken over by the CD ROM and DVD (see later). But there is still significant use being made of videos and they have increased in value for training sessions with the growth in availability of good-quality material. The process is simple and very familiar to many people as a video image projected on the normal type of television receiver or monitor, although large-screen monitors are available and data projectors can project images on to very large screens. Use on the familiar size of monitor is the most common, but this restricts its use to smaller groups.

The video can be used in conjunction with presentations:

- as a stand-alone event in which the video replaces (apart from an introduction) the live presenter;
- at the start of the event to introduce the subject;
- during the presentation at various stages to reinforce the presenter's input, to change the pace and impact of the session or to take the place of part of the presenter's input;
- at the end of the event to act as a recall instrument or to summarize the presentation content;
- after the event, by the participants back at work to recall the messages.

Videos produced for training purposes are much more flexible than the usually accepted format of television programmes and during a presentation can be:

- played straight through, preferably followed by some form of discussion;
- played in the parts required for the supportive purpose;
- interrupted at relevant intervals to involve the group;
- used in a scenario form to trigger discussion.

'Trigger' videos lend themselves well to 'home-made' production and are short cameos of two or three minutes duration in which an event is enacted but not completed. The video is then stopped and the group can be asked questions relating to the scene to extract their views and comments on 'what should happen next'.

The computer – computer-assisted training/learning (CAT/CAL)

The computer is to a large extent the 'Johnny-come-lately' aid on the training scene, but has become invaluable and is increasing in scope and use, perhaps even more so than when the OHP was introduced. As with the video, in some cases the small size of the monitor screen can be a drawback, but a large screen is not always essential. If it is, large-screen projectors are usually available.

Linked with CD ROMs, DVDs and the Internet, the computer's potential use in training is immense. I shall deal with the computer and its allied equipment as a major training process in Chapter 8 (CBT or computer-based training), commenting here only on its role as a training aid and support.

In the simpler use of the computer in training, ie as an aid to the main training process, the computer simply replaces other aids, and uses can include:

- replacing the pre-prepared flipchart;
- replacing the OHP slide;
- replacing the video.

Replacing the pre-prepared flipchart

Pre-prepared flipcharts are used by the trainer to avoid having to write on the chart during the session, risking the bad practice of turning one's back on the group or having periods of silence during writing. The text and graphics of these pre-preparations can be produced as documents on the computer and projected to the group at the relevant time. If a discussion seeking additions or amendments is promoted from this, it is very simple, immediately, to amend the computer-held document and print copies, again immediately.

All the techniques used on flipcharts can be used in this medium, but even more so – varied fonts, varied sizes of type, different colours of type and background, and there is significant ease in using graphics from the thousands of clip-art examples and photographs available. The danger is to try to cram too many different features on one representation, thus defeating the object of the variability.

Replacing the OHP slide

Chapter 5 described the production and use of transparencies or slides for use on the overhead projector. The computer can produce, printed on acetate sheets, similar slides, but with a wider opportunity for impactive effects. However, computer-generated slides need not be converted into OHP transparencies and can be accessible for display in colour on the producing computer (and virtually any other compatible one) with or without magnified enhancement. In this way the computer becomes in effect a self-contained slide projector and the slides can be formed with a consistent background or border, type of formatting – including lettering standardized over the slide series – and the use of colour and graphics.

In the same way that documents can be used when stored on the computer, the slides can be filed in sets on the computer in any order that you wish and used for similar presentations or training programmes in the future, and are available for amendment or updating at any time.

The advantages of this include:

- the facility for presenting the same series of slides on a number of occasions;
- modification of individual slides by editing when data changes or other formats are preferred;
- rearrangement of the slides in between presentations;
- permanent retention of a specific slide series.

There are, of course, disadvantages – what system does not have them? – and these include:

- restriction during the presentation to the logical order of showing the slides as determined before the event;
- constraint to the slide as produced, during the event;
- power supply failure;
- small computer screen visibility.

The first disadvantage is not insurmountable as the programs are usually sufficiently flexible (unless automatic) to return to a previously shown slide, or to skip a slide or two. However, if the presentation is restricted to manual operation to allow for this the often valuable automatic facility has been lost.

Nor is the second disadvantage immutable because, if it becomes known during the presentation that part of a slide is incorrect, the slide *could* be edited. This would not normally be done, however, as it interferes with the flow of the session, much more so than making a simple pen alteration on an OHP slide.

Unless there is an alternative power supply, or the computer is battery operated, little can be done if the power supply fails. Battery-operated computers are usually laptops with a very small screen, hardly usable in a training session or presentation, and transmission to a large-screen projector will require mains power.

The last-mentioned disadvantage is no problem if the learning group is small. If the group is large, provided the facility is available, the computer signals can be sent to a large screen projector, described earlier, whether in the training room itself or with the computer in another room.

CAT/CAL software programs

If the session has been designed so that the trainer is satisfied with the slides and their order, the set of computer-held slides can be inserted (or produced originally) in a software program especially designed for this purpose. An example of this is the widely used *Microsoft PowerPoint* program. In such programs the slides can be filed, in order of playing, into a slide show that can be used by projecting the slides progressively on either the computer screen or a projection screen. The presenter can stand away from the screen, thus obviating any possibility of blocking it with his or her body or part of an OHP, the slides being changed with the click of a mouse.

In addition the normal and obvious facilities are supplemented by additional and useful ones that include:

- *Automatic slide timing* with variable times for different slides, a facility that can be overridden by the trainer/presenter, with or without a prerecorded vocal accompaniment.
- *Slide transitions* with a black image in between slides, the audience's attention being brought back to the speaker (this is a considerable improvement over the OHP, which can have bright, white emptiness between slides if it is not turned off).
- *Slide dissolving* from one to the next, the speed of transition being controllable, and so avoiding the obvious slide change.
- *Slides that build* word by word, or line by line (the OHP slide equivalent of disclosure) and so add movement to what is basically a stationary object. The next word/line appears from the top, bottom or sides of the slide and moves into its correct place, often being highlighted or differently coloured.
- *Hidden slides* that do not automatically display. The decision whether or not to show during a particular presentation is taken prior to the event, depending on such factors as time, the type of audience, confidentiality, and so on, all without actually deleting the slide from the series.
- *Slide branching* to introduce another slide series into the major series if it is decided that this is what is required.
- *Branching to another application* – switching in, for example, a spreadsheet as an up-to-date piece of evidence, part of a report, and so on.
- *Complete and simple control of the running* (and stopping) of the program and other associated programs by the trainer from the computer keyboard or mouse. With these two facilities of the computer complete manual control can be transferred to the trainer.

Programs such as *PowerPoint* that produce computer-generated slides offer a variety of builds, frames and backgrounds, the principal caveat being that you must be careful not to reduce the impact of the slide content with an over-powering background. An example of a slide produced for inclusion in a slide show of this nature is shown in Figure 6.1.

The result of using the computer, whether the image is retained on the computer program or printed using a colour printer, is a very clean, clear, crisp permanent slide that, if retained on the computer, can be revised simply, if this becomes necessary, or duplicated for multi-sets. You can batch the slides in similar subject groups or even have a complete presentation set of slides together in one file. Gone are the days of losing a slide and having to spend hours constructing a new one – the computer offers this facility in a matter of minutes.

Replacing the video

Video programmes, whether complete or of the trigger variety, are held on video cassettes. Exactly the same features are available for playing through the computer, held either on a CD-ROM or on a DVD. The advantages of these are their ease of use, the use of a single machine, condensed filing facilities and, certainly in the case of DVD, improved images. In many cases it is possible to add sequences, images and lettering of your own design to the CD, although copyright clauses have to be watched. An even better advantage is that by using the computer and the Internet, still and video images can be downloaded for immediate or later use. The computer and the Internet are opening up avenues of learning support that were unimagined only a few years ago, and the electronic wizards haven't finished yet!

7

More Than Just Talking

In Chapters 5 and 6 we considered how an input session can be made more interesting and how to help the participants to learn rather than their simply sitting listening to you talk. At the least there was something for them to look at (eg slides on the OHP), and the flipchart could be an aid to recording their contributions, moving them away from a passive to a more active role. In order to extend these benefits further an increase in moving them from passivity to activity is desirable. This can range from a very simple activity, such as the posing of questions by the trainer (discussed in Chapter 3), to substantial case studies and organizational simulations.

As a new trainer it is unlikely that you will become involved in the more complex of these activities, but the quicker you do so the more quickly will you improve the quality of your training and increase the amount of learning achieved by the participants.

Some of these activities are indispensable – buzz groups, syndicates or subgroups, discussions, demonstrations and, of course, questioning. Other more complex activities in which you will eventually engage include case studies and simulations, role playing, exercises/games/activities, using videos actively, computer-assisted training (CAT) and computer-based training (CBT). The more common ones used by new trainers are discussed in detail here, with the others presented in summary form to be researched more fully at a later date when you are approaching the time of using them.

The activities discussed in this chapter are:

- buzz groups;
- syndicates;
- discussions;
- demonstrations;
- question and answer;
- short group activities.

Other, perhaps more substantial ones will be discussed in Chapter 8:

- role playing, including closed-circuit TV;
- case studies and simulations;
- the in-basket or in-tray activity;
- action mazes;
- brainstorming;
- computers (CBT);
- action learning.

Buzz groups

A learning group is commonly broken into subgroups that are sent to separate rooms to discuss, perhaps decide, and report back on a topic. This can be quite a complicated process (see later) and you may have a training session that you do not want to disrupt to this extent, but if you still want to use the technique, albeit in modified form, buzz groups are an answer.

At a prepared point in your session (or extemporarily if you have the skill to cope with this type of situation) you can pose a question to the group or make a statement about part of your subject that you want them to consider. Rather than have them do this as the full group immediately, ask them to break up into sub-groups of three or four people. Rather than have them leave the room, ask them to turn their chairs round to face each other in their sub-groups, or to make up these buzz groups in different parts of the room. The question or statement is then posed and they are given 5 or 10 minutes to discuss and reach some level of conclusion. Each sub-group should appoint one of their number to be the reporter – this is particularly useful early in a course when not all the participants may feel easy about speaking in the full group.

In many cases, particularly in the early stages of the course, the selection of who should go in which buzz group is not important, since the principal purpose of the activity is to encourage the members to start talking and to start developing an active role in the course. There may be occasions, however, when you may wish to select members for each group – say, on a question about the working practices of the sexes, buzz groups of all women; all men; mixed groups with a majority of women/men; balanced mixed groups, and so on.

After the allotted time the buzz groups re-form as the full group. The reporters from each buzz group are asked to give the report from their group, making the point that they are reporting, not as themselves but as the representative of the group – this takes personal pressure from them.

The reason for the title 'buzz' will be obvious while the sub-groups are discussing, particularly if you have four or five sub-groups of four or five people, all talking at the same time.

Syndicates

A training syndicate is an extension of the buzz group concept. It is also referred to as a task sub-group or in the United States (more frequently) as a breakout group. My personal preference is for sub-group as it describes its division from the main group and does not have the wider implications of the other titles! Usually the sub-groups are formed during or following a session to put into practice the learning achieved in the session. They are given separate rooms or, in a very large training room, separate corners, where they can discuss in private and without visual or verbal interruptions, and are give a task or tasks to complete. Following the period allocated they return to the main room where each sub-group is given, in turn, the opportunity to report its findings to the main group.

A common practice is to allow each sub-group to report back uninterrupted, with the trainer summarizing the conclusions of each group on a flipchart. After the final report, the trainer leads a discussion on the results, sub-group members commenting on the findings of the other groups.

An alternative, which can become complex and difficult to control, is to have a discussion after each presentation with a final discussion based on, again, the summarized points recorded by the trainer, or any flipcharts prepared by the sub-groups.

In the case where the sub-groups have each to produce a list, successively reporting groups can be asked to report only on items that previous groups have not described.

The tasks given to the sub-groups can cover the full range of solution seeking, problem solving, decision making; a views and opinions gathering exercise; or a management skill, game or activity. A specific time in which to complete the task is usually given. A tip to ensure full understanding is not to say 'You have 20 minutes to complete this task.' (When does the 20 minutes start – from then or from when they reach their rooms, or after the brief is read, and so on?) Instead say 'You should return to the main room at xx am/pm ready to report back.'

Depending on the stage of the course or the objectives of the session, chairpersons for the sub-groups can be nominated by the trainer, or the sub-groups given the option of electing their own chairperson (or not if they so wish), and of electing a sub-group reporter. The allocation of the chairperson role by the trainer can be useful in certain management skills courses when the objective is to give every participant the opportunity of being a chairperson, the selection following a predetermined pattern over a number of activities.

Discussions

Discussions are very common and powerful learning techniques and situations and occur in a variety of training situations. They can be planned in advance, the preparation including the time, topic, and approach method. Or they can be spontaneous discussions raised from a comment or viewpoint expressed in the session by either the trainer or the learners. A specific session can even be set up as a discussion event alone. The principal value of discussion in a training event is the opportunity not only for the learners to become actively involved and voice their opinions or offer information, but also to bring members into the discussion who have up to then been very low or non-contributors.

The main features of the discussion or discussion group are:

- In a small group there is an atmosphere of willingness to share views and information, and to introduce and develop ideas in what is usually seen by the participants as a relatively safe environment.
- The exchange of views between the members helps them to listen and learn, resulting in a wider and fuller understanding.
- Most people who have come to an event to learn find that they like this approach, and so are more amenable to learning.

Discussion must involve a significant element of planning by the trainer. If it is spontaneous, the trainer must possess the skills of leading a discussion.

The purposes of discussion

Planned or spontaneous discussions have a number of purposes, which include:

- sharing knowledge about a subject;
- presenting and sharing new ideas;
- enabling individual conclusions to be drawn and tested;
- seeking solutions to problems;
- decision making;
- identifying, assessing and recommending attitudes and behaviours;
- a break from the more formal stages of a session or training event;

- developing learning group relationships;
- encouraging learning group members (particularly the quieter members) to express their views, etc;
- having an effect on the individual and group attitudes of the members.

The discussion-leading process

Where the trainer is to be the discussion leader and the introduction of the discussion has been planned, having a process can be of value. One useful and effective format is:

1. Decide on the topic – one that is included within a session or course and would benefit from the discussion approach, or a discrete subject for a discussion.
2. Decide how to launch the discussion:
    - a reference to previously introduced material;
    - a provocative statement;
    - a mystery statement – for example 'three out of five' (marriages end in divorce);
    - an extension of the current subject.
3. Decide on the method of launching the discussion:
    - make a verbal statement from (2);
    - show a visual aid containing a written or graphic statement.
4. Decide on and write down your opening statement, quotation or question – as with the presentation part of input sessions, the start is often the most difficult, so if you write it down and perhaps memorize it you will have one thing less on your mind as you get started.
5. If this is feasible, decide on the seating. A circular arrangement is usually the most effective as everybody can see everybody else and, if you are placed within the circle, you do not dominate as the obvious leader.
6. Make the seating change as naturally as possible. It is usually more acceptable if the chairs are pulled into the circle by the members just before the start of the discussion, rather than the trainer doing this while the group is out of the room – this can make them suspicious and can inhibit the start of discussion.
7. Decide on your own role. This will in most cases be as initiator and prompter during the discussion – more than this and it could turn into another input session. In general, once you have introduced the subject and perhaps given a trigger to start the discussion, your role should be unobtrusive and neutral. Express your own views minimally, unless asked to do so more fully by the group and only then if this will not direct the group in any way. The

discussion is usually held to obtain the views of the members, not your own, although as suggested you may be asked or required to offer them.

8. Identify any special actions you may need to take. You may know, for example, that a particular group may find it difficult to maintain a discussion – keep one or two statements or questions ready to throw into the discussion if it starts to flag, but only do this when it looks as if it is really necessary, to avoid collapse. You may know that certain members will try to dominate or avoid the discussion – decide how you will try to control the former or bring in the latter, unless the group do so themselves.

9. Decide whether you are going to challenge incomplete, unclear or false contributions or are going to leave it to the members themselves (even if they fail to do so). Consider strategies to encourage the inter-member challenges during the discussion. Comments on any failures to challenge can be brought out in the subsequent review of the discussion.

10. End the discussion when it has obviously reached this stage or when time is up, and ensure that either you make a summary of what has happened/ been decided or, preferably, that this is made by one of the discussion group members.

11. Lead a very informal discussion and feedback of the event.

A discussion-leading brief

If one of your decisions about a discussion is that you will be the discussion leader and, although taking a minimally active role, will be unobtrusively in control of its comprehensiveness and content, or if you are going to take an active lead, you will need some form of discussion-leading brief in the same way as an input or presentation session. This will obviously not be as extensive as the presentation brief but it will serve the same purpose, ie it will remind you of the topics that should be/must be covered during the period. The two main forms of discussion-leading brief are the shopping list and the pros and cons list. Which one you use will depend on your personal preferences and also on the complexity of the subject to be discussed.

The shopping list

This is a simple reminder list, laid out in whichever format suits you best (vertical, horizontal, patterned). It includes key words that will remind you of the subjects that should be discussed during the event – the training technique of 'Must Knows, Should Knows and Could Knows' can be very useful here. As the discussion progresses, the items satisfactorily covered can be struck off the list, the remainder acting as a reminder of what else should be discussed. This is particularly useful when the discussion falters and subjects still on the list can be raised with the group.

The pros and cons list

When you consider as a possibility or know that the subject to be discussed will arouse a lot of controversy and/or will be complex, with different members taking differing and opposing views, a pros and cons list can be produced prior to the discussion. This will include, in a summarized form, as many of the subject aspects and arguments as you are able to identify.

Divide an A4 sheet of paper vertically as shown in Figure 7.1.

PROs	CONs

Figure 7.1 A pros and cons list

List as many of the aspects and arguments as you can in their relevant columns. During the discussion, as with the shopping list, strike through subjects covered effectively and use the remainder, not only as simple reminders of subjects to be covered, but also as a checklist of the main arguments that should emerge.

Both these approaches should help you to keep track of the progress of the discussion. They will also ensure that all the significant topics have been covered, and to the extent necessary.

Demonstrations

Demonstrations are a particularly useful technique for use in a session that is concerned with training in the knowledge and skills of a technical object or subject – using a machine, gaining a clerical or machine skill, using computer hardware or software, and so on. Demonstrations add additional interest to a presentation and link very well with the 'Tell, show, do' approach. Obviously much will depend on the size or mobility of the object, but the demonstration can form a useful part of the introduction to the session, or be used progressively as the session develops.

Demonstrations of more general or 'soft' skills, such as people skills, are more difficult, and in fact may present dangers. If the demonstration is, for example, of a negotiation, there is the danger that the observing learners will see this as 'this is the way you *must* do it'. If the demonstration 'fails', the credibility of the approach becomes suspect in the minds of the learners, even if the 'failure' was due to the demonstrator rather than the process.

The opposite approach, of an incorrect demonstration, is much safer, giving the learner group the opportunity to identify 'what' went wrong and 'why', leading on to how the approach could be improved.

Question and answer

Some of the techniques for asking questions within a session have been discussed in Chapter 5, and have been recommended as a simple and useful method of introducing more activity into the session. Whichever approach is used – establishing facts, eliciting feelings, identifying values – it must be handled with care, as too easily the questioning can become or seem to be an interrogation or even a put-down of the responders. The friendly approach is advocated and is exemplified by questions that lead from facts to feelings and values – 'What do you think?', 'Why do you think that?', 'How deeply do you think about that?', 'Would you do it any differently?', and so on.

Questions can also be from the learning group to the trainer, but sometimes the group has to be encouraged to ask them, particularly in the early stages of a course. The trainer's advice to the group on when they can ask questions has been mentioned earlier, but this must not be done in a way that will actively discourage them. Some approaches that can be used to help include:

● Make sure the group know when they can ask questions – during the session or at the end.
● If the decision is to keep questions until the end, encourage them to make notes of the questions they want to ask as the session progresses.
● A risky ploy, but if you suspect that the group may find it difficult to start the questioning, arrange with one of the learners whom you know well to start the questioning.
● Ask yourself a reflective question to start the process, such as 'One of the questions that I am often asked is "Why. . . ?"'

- Ask the group a specific question when you have a good idea that there will be a reaction, for example 'Did anyone disagree with the part of my material that dealt with. . . and when I suggested. . . ?'
- Sit out the silence – who knows, they may break before you do!

Listening to the questions and answers

A major failing among trainers who ask the group a question when they know the answer themselves is to fail to make the most of a question period by do not listening to the answers. In the other direction, trainers' responses to a question from the group can be less than satisfactory for the same reason – they do not fully listen to the question. So:

- Listen carefully to either the question or answer and make sure that you understand it. If not, ask a clarifying question.
- If the question or response is long and complex do not be afraid of making notes of the key points.
- Restate the question or answer, if necessary in a summarized form – this gives you time to consider it and how you are going to respond. However, do not use this technique too often or too frequently as the group will quickly identify what you are doing and name you 'the parrot'.
- When responding to a question do so as concisely as possible, being as comprehensive as possible. But do not worry unduly if you do not say everything you wanted to say; if the original questioner wants more they will ask a supplementary question.

Some 'don'ts'

Don't:

- Be defensive when the learner questioner is aggressive, appears to be questioning your professionalism or credibility, or when the subject is controversial.
- Enter into a dialogue that lasts too long with the person who has asked the question – you will lose the remainder of the group.
- Be too speedy to answer the question – it is only too easy when rushing in to give an incorrect answer or say things you didn't mean to. Pause, think about the question (this will be appreciated), answer only then.
- Try to put down the questioner either by saying something in a patronizing manner or in an embarrassing way, or by your non-verbal communication giving the impression that you think the questioner is simple or stupid.
- Try to answer a question to which you do not know the answer. Admit this, but promise to find out the answer as soon as possible – and do so.

- Try to answer more than one question at the same time – for example when two people ask different questions almost simultaneously. Confirm that you realize they both want answers, ask one to hold the question until you have dealt with the other – and remember to go back to the other person.
- Ask more than one question yourself at the same time – the group will be confused about which one to try to answer.
- Ask questions you know the group can't answer, with the objective of demonstrating your own superiority.

Short group activities

I believe that when you are working with a group of learners, although input of new material is important, the real learning takes place when they are engaged in an activity – interacting with each other, solving a problem, or practising the skills that have been introduced by the input session or other means. There is little point in exuding knowledge to the group and leaving it at that, expecting them to return to their work skilled in that topic. In the learning cycle the process begins with an experience, whether this is an activity or an input, and the remainder of the learning involves considering this experience in various ways.

Practical events, that is, experiential events in which the learners participate, are described variously and often rather loosely as exercises, games or activities, the choice often being one of personal preference. However, to me 'exercises' is reminiscent of the classroom or the gym; 'games' does not have a serious ring to it, although sometimes what is needed in a course is a non-serious game. For me the word 'activity' suggests all these types of events.

The features of an activity

Activities have a number of basic features:

- They provide vehicles for learning, with the learners *doing* something from which the relevant lessons can be drawn.
- The experience can be based on a real-life situation, an artificially produced event or an artificial event constructed from, for example, a case brought by one of the learners.
- Appropriate activities can be selected to suit the learning event, the learners, the environment, the numbers involved and the time available.

- The learners, either as the full learning group or divided into sub-groups, perform the event either in their own personae or in selected roles.
- The details of the event are summarized in a brief or set of briefs that might be detailed or simply summaries from which the learners can develop an appropriate role.
- The activity can be observed in a range of ways.
- Generally, learners enjoy taking part in activities and consequently the likelihood of learning is enhanced.
- They can be used as learning activities, introductions, icebreakers or session shakers.

Disadvantages

Although in general activities have a significant place in the training plan, they do have some disadvantages. This is particularly the case for the new trainer, since to step away from the power position of controlling the session through an activity gives the learners a lot of power themselves. This can be disconcerting, if not frightening, for a new trainer whose previous experience may have been simply presenting a set input session. However, if you bite the bullet and become involved in learning through activity, you will not only see that the participants can learn substantially from the experience, but both you and they will enjoy what is happening. Some of the disadvantages are:

- There is a danger that too many activities are included in a programme, with the result that it might come to be known as the 'game show'.
- Not all learners will learn, or will want to learn, from the activity approach.
- Some learners might see the activity as 'playing silly games'.

In my training experience I have encountered both of the last two. The situation has usually been saved by, in the first case, achieving the learning from the reflection and theorizing stages, and in the latter, by ensuring that the lessons from the 'silly game' can be translated and applied to a real work situation.

Activity uses

There are three principal uses for short activities in training and development programmes:

- introductory activity;
- icebreaker;
- energizer or session shaker.

Introductory activity

Every training course, however short, benefits from some form of introduction and, if there is time, a participant introduction activity at the start. Whatever form of introduction activity is used, although the emergent information is useful and important, the real importance of the activity is getting the learners involved from an early stage.

Introductory activities include:

- the traditional 'creeping death', in which, in turn, the members introduce themselves, either on a free basis or following topic guidelines suggested by the trainer;
- the 'Russian roulette' variation of the 'creeping death', in which the trainer nominates, at random, the order in which the learners should introduce themselves;
- paired interviewing and introductions where, in pairs, the learners interview each other then introduce their partner to the full group;
- progressive group introductions, in which learners within small groups introduce themselves, then change groups and repeat the process, until everybody has been introduced to everybody else;
- identity maps in which the learners draw pictures illustrating their lives and careers and use these to introduce themselves;
- identity wheels, which have segments requiring the entry of information by the learners about themselves.

It is all too easy for the trainer to select the 'creeping death' approach, even when there is time to include something more adventurous, but this is the introduction activity that is least enjoyed by the learners and is usually the least effective approach.

Any introductory activity is introduced immediately following the domestic introduction to the course and although seemingly simple and straightforward, it has to be planned carefully. From the trainer's point of view it is beneficial to the session or course that: a) the members start to get to know each other, b) they start to interact with each other, and c) they have an early opportunity to start contributing to the event. But the learners may not appreciate these factors and may react against an introduction because they 'want to get on with the learning'. This could be particularly relevant in a short event and consequently the trainer must select what appears to be the most suitable activity in terms of content and the length of time it takes. Every one of the introductory activities mentioned above takes time away from the 'meat' of the session or course, but their value has to be weighed against this expenditure of time. The actual time taken will depend on:

- the extent of the material to be covered in the introductory activity – simple exchange of names; exchange of more substantial personal details; inclusion of such aspects as attitudes, opinions and feelings; identification of expectations and concerns, and so on;
- the time available within the session or course – courses can have a duration of half a day, a full day, two or three days, several days, or longer.

Literally hundreds of these introductory activities exist, many contained in published resource packs, others on CD ROMs, yet others (both free and for sale) on a number of Web sites (private and commercial), and many (some original, some modified from public activities) held in the training departments of organizations. There are in fact so many that if you could only identify where the activity that most suits your needs can be found you would never need to 'invent' one.

Icebreakers

Icebreakers are activities that link closely with introductory activities and merge frequently, particularly as they are often described as introductory. They are usually short, say five minutes, or can be substantially longer; they can be humorous ('to break the ice'), or little more than party games. Icebreakers can be merged with an introductory activity or can follow one.

Icebreakers intended to follow up the introductory activity generate action in the learners and continue the process of enabling them to relate with each other, opening up even further their reactions to each other. The introductions have started the process of encouraging the learners to divulge information about themselves; the icebreaker continues and develops this process.

Two types of icebreaker exist: one for the purpose described above, the other much simpler, in that it aims to make the participants feel easier with each other.

The latter activity can take almost any form, many of which have no relation to work or to the training. This type of activity can be a simple problem-solving one or can be a much deeper one involving the development of trust by means of a 'trust walk'. Quizzes held in sub-groups are common in this context; they encourage cooperation, but in an atmosphere of fun, and may also be used as a discreet method of identifying the participants' knowledge.

The more serious icebreakers try to enable further information about the participants to emerge. An example of this is the expectations or hopes/concerns chart on page 53.

Energizers or session shakers

Energizers, or session shakers, are generally simple activities, short and sharp, that usually have no relationship to the programme objectives. They can be introduced at any time during a programme, the trigger usually being a flagging energy level within the learning group.

In the same way as other training activities, they should be planned for as far as possible. But you can keep yourself prepared by having a set of these activities in your 'toolbox'. Just as we find with introductory and icebreaker activities, energizers abound in the resource literature and on Web sites.

The occasions on which you will find an energizer most useful will include:

- Immediately after a lunch break when the group re-forms and their eyes have that 'heavy' look. An energizer is much more rewarding than an input session at this time, usually referred to as the 'pudding session'.
- After a heavy, serious, but essential input when the group appears to be finding the learning hard going and a practical break would help.
- At the start of the second and subsequent training days of an extended programme – in such cases the learners look forward to these inconsequential breaks from serious learning and frequently start asking for them.
- When the session has been a physical one, the activity can require the group to sit down and take part in a mental activity. Or the reverse can apply, an energizer being physical when the learners have been steeped in mental activity.
- When there is a major change in the subject of a course and it is useful to break the learners' chain of thoughts from the previous topic.

Many session shakers have their origins in children's or party games, or variations of physical education exercises. Several are variations of competitive relay activities – for example words on cards taken across a room to the remainder of the team by a member hopping. When something has been done with this word, another member hops across the room to pick up another word and return to the team.

The same caveat for these types of activities must be kept in mind as for the other ones described previously – insert them into the programme judiciously and do not overuse them, as too frequent a use can have a negative effect.

8

More Training
Activity Approaches

In Chapter 7 we started to consider how an input session can be made more interesting and help the participants to learn, rather than their simply sitting listening to you talk, by introducing some form of activity. The activities described were of the shorter type; in this chapter the activities involve a more substantial and time-consuming resource, but they are common in pragmatic, experiential learning events.

The activities discussed in this chapter are:

- substantial learning group activities;
- role playing, including closed-circuit TV;
- case studies and simulations;
- the in-tray or in-basket activity;
- action mazes;
- brainstorming;
- computers (CBT);
- action learning.

Learning activity

Learning is usually the main use of an activity during a training and development programme. A learning activity is used to:

- Assess the existing or developed skills of the learners by direct observation of them performing a task. This can be used as an initial assessment of pre-learning skills, interim development and terminal skills at the end of the learning event.

- Demonstrate, prior to more defined learning approaches, learning points about the subject under consideration, eg an activity prior to a detailed input session to enable the learners to identify the level of their existing knowledge and skills.
- Consolidate, through practice, learning that has been achieved prior to the activity in some other form of training approach, eg an input session.

These uses immediately suggest that there can be more than one activity, at different times, within a training session. For example, a training session might follow a pattern of:

1. A full discussion of the activity and the learning points for the session.
2. A brief input introduction to the subject by the trainer, including a general description and statement of learning objectives.
3. An activity related to the session material to demonstrate and assess the level of the learners' knowledge and skill at this stage.
4. An input of the new material by the trainer, using relevant audio and visual aids and encouraging active participation by the learners through questioning and discussion.
5. At relevant point(s) during the session, mini activities might be held to clarify particular points, eg by means of buzz groups.
6. An activity, based on real life or artificially produced, to consolidate the learning and enable the learners to practise the learning points.

Forms of activities

One form of activity is completely artificial, being 'constructed', eg a problem-solving exercise, which has no relationship to the work of the learning group, or even to work itself – for example, the classical NASA activity in which a group is assumed to have crash-landed on the moon with a variety of articles. The problem to be solved is the prioritization of these in such a situation.

This type has no immediate relationship to the work culture or environment, but the lessons to be drawn from the activity and the way in which the solution is approached are totally applicable to the event objectives and to the working situation. The NASA scenario obviously has no relationship to the likely experience of any of us except perhaps astronauts, and the likelihood of similar circumstances arising for them is also highly unlikely. Although the actual situation in which the problem-solving group finds itself is unreal, there are very real lessons that can be drawn from its process and applied to almost any working situation. These include the skills of:

analysis

problem solving

team building

individual behaviour

identification of value judgements
   and life attitudes

planning

decision making

group behaviour

assertiveness

communication; and so on.

The second form of activity is one in which, for example, the problem to be solved is an actual work one, either one that has already been solved (and the group's approach can be weighed against the real-life decision) or one that is current and for which no solution has yet been found. An interim type of such an activity would be a hypothetical, but realistic, work problem that has not yet arisen but could arise. Any of these could be posed for the group's discussion, and related to the learning points.

Planning and design

The primary reason for using an activity is that it is directly related to the objectives of the learning programme, not just an amusing interlude. An activity rarely stands alone as the learning vehicle, rather it acts as a strong support for the more formal approach to the learning – an input session, video, or computer program – and is used in conjunction with these. Many types of activity require a substantial amount of time so there must be considerable planning for their inclusion.

Timing

Most significant activities also require a substantial amount of time for their performance. 'Performance' obviously includes briefing, doing and reviewing. Few structured group activities that have worthwhile results can be performed in under about 45 minutes, and the majority can take much longer. Typically the briefing (if any observers are not to have substantial preparation) can take about 10 minutes, the activity itself a minimum of 20 minutes and the review period, which depends of course on the method used and the number of sub-groups, at least 30 minutes. One aspect that is often forgotten in planning the time to be allotted is the time that the groups take to go to their syndicate rooms and return to the main room at the end of the activity. A straightforward approach such as this quickly adds up to 70 minutes or so, a substantial part of a training day.

Grouping

Using activities during a training course usually requires the sub-groups to be selected in some way. This can be a completely random approach but frequently, if there are to be a number of activities during the course, a system of rotation of the group members must be decided. It is worth remembering that this may not be a simple affair with little significance. Typical comments by learners after a series of activities can include:

- 'Why did I have to change groups? I was getting along so well with that group.'
- 'Why did we have to stay in the same group all the time? I didn't like the other members and I wanted to work with other people.'
- 'I would have liked to have stayed with the group of people from my organization so we could relate the situations to our culture.'
- 'I would have liked to have been in different groups with people from other organizations. I'm sure they have different approaches to the ones we have.'

There are several reasons why the grouping might need to be changed during the event. It may be that a group of high contributors/reactors are not learning from being included in one sub-group, in spite of their behaviour being reviewed. Consequently, because the event objectives are concerned with behaviour, the trainer might decide to repeat and open up the learning opportunity by having the same group of people together again (and again?).

If the learning involves reinforcing a new technique that has different applications in different organizations represented on the event, it makes sense to group familiars and if necessary maintain that grouping.

Structured group activities can suggest the whole spectrum of learner groupings, again with the decision dominated by the needs of the programme linked to those of the learning group. If a number of opportunities to practise similar techniques, or progressive parts of such techniques, is provided, care must be taken to ensure that as many learners as possible can take the major learning roles. This can be achieved mainly by a predetermined rota system.

Other groupings, depending on the learning event needs, can be random. In such cases I have used 'even numbers round the group for one group'; for the next activity, 'odd numbers round the group'; for the next one alternately seated members, and so on. Not scientific, but it has the advantage of simplicity, as long as you remember which system you used previously.

Where the population of sub-groups has no major influence on the event a most satisfactory approach is to give the learners the responsibility for:

- choosing their first groups;
- deciding whether to maintain these groups after one or two activities;
- with guidance and advice, deciding which grouping will most serve their needs.

Resources

Activities require as much planning and preparation as an input session and frequently almost as many resources. Every activity requires:

- briefs for the participants (unless the introduction is so simple that it can be given verbally);
- briefs for the observers (if these are used separately from the participants);
- rooms for the sub-groups, or their own private space in a single large room;
- relevant materials related to the specific activity;
- support material – paper, pens, flipcharts, markers, etc. One aspect on which many trainers fall down is the provision of flipchart paper and markers. It is so easy for the learners to use more paper than was estimated and they almost invariably bring the markers back to the main room and forget to return them!

Each activity may require different resources, so it is very helpful to have a file for each activity you plan to include in the learning event. Keep these in order of use and in each folder include:

- the required number of briefs for the number of learners (plus one or two extra as contingency copies);
- the required number of activity briefs and observer briefs for the number of observers to be used;
- a checklist of the method of running the activity, including a clear statement of any instructions to be given verbally;
- a checklist of resources required, as described above;
- a checklist of the essential learning points that must be brought out in the review, whichever method is used.

Final preparation

Once the various decisions suggested above have been made, the time is approaching for the final preparations to include the activity. These should include:

1. Be as familiar as possible with the activity – its form, timing, operation, review and feedback.
2. If the activity is new to you, try it out with a group of colleagues or other 'safe' group.
3. Produce the necessary briefs, instruction sheets, observation and review/ feedback instruments.
4. Check that you have any other resources required for the activity.
5. If the activity is physical, confirm that it is suitable for the particular group.
6. If relevant, decide how you are going to form the activity sub-groups.
7. Check that you have sufficient space for a group to perform the activity, and/or additional rooms if multiple sub-groups are to be involved.
8. Check any necessary safety factors.
9. Confirm the activity timings – this can be done in conjunction with (2) above, bearing in mind that experienced trainers might perform the activity more quickly than learners.
10. Prepare your verbal introduction for the activity.
11. Decide on the observation strategy and methods.
12. Decide what role you will take during the activity.
13. Decide the methods for reviewing the activity and giving feedback.

Briefs and instruction sheets

Many activities are too complex for a simple verbal introduction to be sufficient. This means that role briefs or individual and group instruction sheets should be provided for the participants at the start of the activity.

The preparation of effective briefs is not easy. If they are long and complex understanding may be impeded; if they are short and snappy there may be insufficient information to help the participants. The dummy-run recommended above should help you to achieve a balance, although the 'ineffectiveness' of the brief will always be used as an excuse by participants who 'fail' in an activity.

Role playing

This is one of the most widely used activities in training courses and provides the learners with the opportunity to practise, in simulated conditions that can be made as close to real life as possible, the learning they have hopefully achieved. Role plays can be either linked with or integral parts of input sessions concerned with a range of subjects – interviews for counselling, grievance, discipline, appraisal, selection, termination – and situations in which more than two people are involved, such as negotiations. Role plays are usually related to interview training as outlined above, one learner taking the part of the interviewer (eg a manager), the other the part of the interviewee (eg member of staff), but roles can be carried out in syndicate groups, case studies and simulations.

The value of role plays if conducted carefully and simulated as closely as possible to real life is that the learners can practise newly learnt techniques in a safe environment and have feedback – the latter is rare in real life, but is essential to let the learner know how well they are succeeding. The environment of the session in the training course is safe and apart from giving the learners confidence also allows them to experiment with techniques or approaches, experiments that would be dangerous in the real-life interview.

Role plays can be developed from real-life cases that have occurred in the learners' organizations (names and places being changed to protect the originators of the cases) or the learners can be asked to provide details of cases of which they are aware or in which they have been involved. The latter is particularly valuable as it gives an individual the opportunity, having learnt new techniques, to 'repeat' the interview, avoiding any mistakes of the original one. A useful twist is to have the case 'owner' act as the interviewee, thus giving a view from the other side of the fence.

Variations to the standard role play

There are a number of planned variations possible with role plays depending on the circumstances within the programme, including:

- *Reverse role play* where the original interviewer in real life becomes the interviewee. The practice can show him or her how the original interviewee may have seen their approach.
- *Ghosting or doubling* in which, at stages during an interview, or if the interviewer seems to be losing his or her way, the trainer or another learner stands behind the interviewer and carries on the interview for a period until the original interviewer is ready to continue. If the trainer takes the part of the 'ghost' at times, the impression of 'taking over as the expert' must be avoided, otherwise the learners might become too reliant on the trainer.
- *Empty-chair role playing* in which the problem owner starts by describing to an empty chair opposite them the problem as they see it, discussing all its aspects and raising solutions. They then move between their own chair and the empty chair conducting a 'dialogue' with themselves. This can be a powerful method of airing and solving a problem once the participant becomes immersed in the approach.

The planner must also agree whether a training group is to be divided into smaller groups to practise the role plays, or whether role plays should take place in front of the rest of the group (as, for example, in presentation skills training). The former approach saves time with multiple events taking place simultaneously; but the latter, although more expensive in time, offers a wider range of review feedback, albeit putting stress on the role players who have to enact the roles in front of an audience.

Review and feedback

A particularly important aspect of role plays is the detailed review and feedback of the role performance. Substantial amounts of time have to be built into the programme as the reviews and discussion can be longer than the actual role plays. They can be performed profitably within the role-playing pair and their observer, a final roundup of learning taking place in a plenary session.

A number of approaches to the observation of role plays and the feedback process are possible, the observation area being key, as is it in many activities. The options, many of which will depend on the time available, include:

● role plays by two learners in front of the whole group, observation for eventual feedback being made by the learning group and the trainer;
● role plays by the full learning group simultaneously in pairs with no observers, reliance being placed on the learners to note their own processes, give feedback to each other, then report in plenary;
● in triads, the third member acting as the observer and eventual giver of feedback to the other two, with a final report in plenary;
● any of the above approaches, but also using CCTV to record the interview, supplemented on occasions by an observer.

The most effective and time-saving approach is for the review to take place immediately following the event, the interviewer and interviewee's observer giving the feedback and conducting a review discussion with them. Again this can be occurring simultaneously with every role play event that has been taking place, the trainer(s) moving round the groups to ensure that all is going well. At the end of the reviews the full group can reconvene for a plenary session at which a discussion can take place on the points that have arisen in the sub-group reviews. Obviously, if these reviews are to be worthwhile, they can take up a lot of time and this must be planned for in the session preparation.

The use of CCTV, although highly desirable, introduces significant additional time requirements and complicated processes if more than one role play is taking place at the same time.

Case studies

Case studies (and simulations) can be significant aids to learning, either as complete learning events or, more usually, as activities linked to other parts of the training. In the latter case an input session or series of linked sessions is commonly followed by a case study that, as real-life example, or as an artificially constructed study, contains the opportunity for the learners to practise the learning points that have been covered. They can be similar to syndicate problem-solving activities in that the learners are given a statement of information that contains a problem they are required to solve.

In a major case study a complete historical record of the background of the organization or events is provided, often including material that is not necessary for the performance of the task, but always including the material through which the task might be completed. The closer the data is to the real event the more acceptable will be the study, with errors and omissions less likely.

From the historical data the learners are presented with a problem to be solved, with additional, revised or newer data being made available as necessary. The learning groups make recommendations for the solution of the problem. These recommendations can be presented to and discussed with:

- the trainer;
- other learning groups that have considered the case study at the same time;
- a subject expert;
- an invited line manager with knowledge of the case (where it is real).

Case studies of a complex nature are very suitable for inclusion at the end of a training event, for example on group leadership, the study requiring the learners to practise all the aspects of leadership that have been covered and may have been practised individually or in syndicate groups. Such a major case study can require a substantial period of time to perform and frequently an even longer period for the following review and feedback session.

Planning and design of case studies

The planning requirements for a case study include:

- the decision on whether to use an artificial or a real problem;
- how far the study will extend – a complete organizational problem, specific managerial problems, or personal value situations;
- the resources to be made available – a written brief, a video clip (commercially or home-made), or a computer application;

- whether observers will be used, how and to what extent;
- the role to be taken by the trainer(s) during the activity;
- the format of the review.

Reports, organization charts, job descriptions and so on may all be needed in considerable quantities, and may need modification to make them more suitable for training purposes. Trainers who use case studies of this nature usually find that they spend a lot of time producing the initial study that can then, with only amendments or updates, last for a long time.

Timing

Case studies can be relatively simple and consequently reasonably short in the time required (although rarely as short as the structured activity), or complex and requiring a long period of time. If, in the latter case, the material and the required activity are particularly extensive and complex the study activity can be broken down into stages, perhaps ones that might relate to the progress of the learning programme. For example, one stage might be concerned with the collection and analysis of data, another with problem solving and solution generation, a third with decision making and implementation.

Your preparation time will almost certainly be longer than with the structured activity. The objectives and 'answers' to the short, structured activity are usually relatively simple and require a minimum of review by you prior to it. However, because of the complexity of case studies, the objectives and possible results can be equally complex. You will need to be absolutely clear about the objectives of the study and to have considered all the possible options that could be suggested, the ones that would be more favourable and the reasons for these choices. This should not be so that you can disagree with the results produced by the learners, but you may have to suggest that they reconsider or consider other options.

Your selection of the sub-groups (if these are used) will possibly need to be more discreet than with general structured group activities. Because there may be financial, operational, production and administrative information and problems in the study, if at all possible each group should include a learner who is knowledgeable (or more knowledgeable than the rest) in these topics. Otherwise, a balanced selection according to attitudes and observed behaviour might be the way to proceed.

Simulations

Simulations are usually extensions of the case study, involving the allocation of almost real-life roles, the use of computers and the completion of reports, and meetings requiring problem solving and decision making. Individuals within the group are given, or select, the roles of managing director or chief executive, financial director, sales and marketing director, directors of production, personnel and training and so on. The group is given a time in which to solve a number of problems, or otherwise exist as a company with the objective of making a profit over a sum given to them at the start. Many variations of this type of simulation are possible and the time allocation can be varied very extensively. Consequently, planning for simulations will certainly have to be made during the programme planning phase and may represent a complete learning programme.

A substantial amount of the planning time for a simulation is taken up in writing the case or modifying an existing one to suit the particular circumstances, possibly involving visits to line locations to observe functions and interview job holders, in addition to collecting and collating reports, critical incident reviews, etc. This information is included in the complete simulation as written briefs, reports, minutes and computer program data – so that everything necessary for the effective performance of the activity is available for the learners.

Preparation activity must include the printing and recording of the information and data referred to above and, if observers are to be used, observational aid instruments for these learners. Similarly, many cases and simulations require a number of rooms and a variety of equipment — typewriters, paper, computers, calculators – and plans must be made for these to be available.

The simulation is certainly one occasion where a dummy run with a guinea-pig group can be most worthwhile, not only to iron out problems but to assess the time required. As with the majority of training and development events, a review and feedback session must be planned. This session will obviously be a substantial one and can be a separate occasion, say the following week; half a day or even a day, depending on the complexity of the case, being allocated to the event.

The in-tray or in-basket activity

This is a form of case study that simulates a 'typical' office in-tray (sometimes referred to as an in-basket) with a variety of contents for action. These contents can vary widely – reports, memoranda, notes, requests for information, requests for interviews, invitations, letters and so on. The purpose of the activity is to have the learners sort these items according to learnt criteria and, where necessary, take action. Time for the activity is restricted – as it would be in real life – putting consequent stress on the participants.

The in-tray contents are related to the subjects included in the learning programme. For example, if the programme is concerned with negotiation skills training, most of the in-tray contents will have a negotiation bias.

The activity can be performed with or without observers, most frequently without as it is basically an individual exercise that can be assessed to a large extent by the results. Options can include performing the activity on an individual basis, or with individuals in sub-groups or teams, or as a group exercise.

As with most activities timing will vary with the number of learners involved and the complexity of the activity, but in this case the activity will be planned to last the minimum time possible. This must, however, be a reasonable length and, with a newly created activity, will need to be determined through trial and error.

Objectives

The activity is centred around a number of documents related to the objectives of the exercise. These objectives will need to be clear from the start, although usually this type of activity has fairly specific objectives. The objectives for an in-tray activity include:

- learning and practising the systematic, speedy reading and understanding of a variety of written communications;
- effective analysis of the documents inspected;
- identification of the documents in terms of:
  - urgency;
  - importance;
  - urgency but not importance;
  - importance but not urgency;
  - neither urgency nor importance;
- deciding from the classification which items need to be dealt with and how this should be done;
- taking the decided action in the most appropriate way – writing a memo, making a phone call, making a personal visit;
- keeping effective records of action taken.

The collection of documents placed in the in-tray, other than for specific learning situations, could include:

- complex reports for the next senior management or board meeting (say in three weeks time);
- conflicting time or resource demands;
- decisions required – urgent, etc;
- invitations – to meetings, social functions, talks, association meetings;
- letters – internal, external;
- queries;
- requests for information – simple, complex;
- simple internal memos – from boss, from staff, from peers.

In order to reflect to a major extent the real-life situation and also to introduce a significant element of stress and urgency, a further factor is added. This is that the in-tray decisions must be made in a specific period of time because the manager:

- as owner of the in-tray, is leaving to attend a week-long meeting in another city;
- is going on holiday for two weeks in a remote area where he or she will not be accessible;
- is going into hospital for an operation, will be there for two weeks, including convalescence, during which time he or she must not be contacted.

The procedure for using an in-tray activity would therefore follow lines similar to these:

1. Introduce the activity in general terms, describing briefly the objectives and methods.
2. Divide the learning group into groups of individuals or groups as necessary.
3. Issue each participant or group (in the third method) with a set of the in-tray contents.
4. Brief observers if they are being used.
5. State the time at which the activity will terminate.
6. Commence the activity:
   (a) individuals completing their own in-tray;
   (b) individuals completing their own in-tray, followed by a meeting of the group to discuss, argue and decide on a final group decision;
   (c) the groups completing, as groups, the in-tray decisions.
7. Review the activity.

Action mazes

In an action maze each individual learner is given an information sheet that describes a technical, people or interpersonal problem and asked to make a decision on the facts available at that stage – usually a multiple choice is given. The particular choice leads the learner to the next piece of information and so on, until the final result is reached.

Each learner can proceed at his or her own pace, the aim being to move through the maze to the end solution in the smallest number of moves. An individual who has a good grasp of the principles involved in the type of problem presented can reach the solution quickly, having made the correct choices along most of the pathways. The unskilled learner is likely to make a number of inappropriate choices and be forced to take a circuitous path to the end (if they ever reach it).

The objective of the exercise is for the learners to absorb the correct methods or attitudes from consideration of the mistakes they made. This will, of course, be helped by a review following the activity, in which the reasons for correct and incorrect choices are discussed.

Two principal disadvantages are found in action mazes:

- The 'clever' learner who may have read and absorbed as data the right books and consequently can give the 'right' answers, whether or not the real reasons behind these are understood.
- The activity requires a lot of sheets of paper – a set containing sheets for each of the stages and a set for each participant.

The computer has eased the second disadvantage as a program can be written easily with the 'sheets' as on-screen pages that can be called up from the choices made. The problem with this approach is that a number of computers are required or each participant must have his or her own monitor on a network to the trainer's master computer.

Brainstorming

This technique is used both within training and development and in working situations; it utilizes the technique that has the overall description and aim of creativity. The technique can be used during input sessions, discussions, activities, case studies – whenever the generation of a lot of ideas is required. The principle is that the participants allow their minds to 'freewheel' and make suggestions on a subject, some of which will be old and tried, some completely new, others apparently rather silly and yet others completely unworkable. I say 'apparently rather silly' as, when they are looked at, some may turn out to be the most effective solution or suggestion. After all, who would have thought logically about a bouncing bomb to destroy the Moehne Dam? Why did a wine press give Gutenberg the idea for a printing press?

The process belies the concept of freewheeling creativity, as it follows a strict pattern of a leader introducing the topic, inviting suggestions, not allowing interruptions or explanations, encouraging further suggestions and summarizing, at intervals, the suggestions made as the brainstorm proceeds. A recorder notes *every suggestion* made, however apparently silly or unworkable, and helps the leader in interim and final summaries. The participants are encouraged to come up with as many suggestions, ideas and proposals as they can, without describing them or having disagreement or argument voiced about them. The purpose of the rules, for example no interruptions, is to enable people to think freely rather than have their minds directed along a singular path.

At the end of the brainstorm (after a predetermined time or when ideas dry up completely) the list of suggestions is analysed (by the same or a different group) into:

- Previously used or suggested and rejected ideas. Circumstances may have changed and what was once a non-acceptable idea might now be realistic.
- Attractive and possibly workable ideas, particularly if they are completely new and novel, but not over the top.
- Unusual ideas that may work – who knows?
- Obviously unworkable ideas, but rejected only when it is absolutely certain that they would not work (at that time).

From the analysis a final selection of the best solution(s) is made for submission to the person who has raised the question.

Within a training event it is common, rather than having the brainstorm in the full training group, to divide the learning group into several sub-groups. The findings of the sub-groups are then combined in a plenary session. The learning group is again subdivided to consider and recommend the finally acceptable ideas and, again, return to the plenary session to agree the whole group's decisions.

Computers (CBT)

The use of computers in training has been described earlier under CAT and also when more traditional training approaches were being discussed. The computer generally facilitates the speed and ease of the activity. But the computer is also used in training in its own right, the training being based on computer use. CBT can be used in a traditional environment with a group of learners or, increasingly, on an individual, self-learning basis with trainer support only (this is discussed in Chapter 9). The use of computers in/as training could be a significant learning force in the future.

The earlier CBT approaches were customarily computer packages usually contained on CD ROMs, then interactive CD ROMs and, more recently, DVDs. These are often supported by, or themselves support, text and/or video material, projects and a range of activities.

Advantages
The advantages of the CBT package include:

● The learners take part in an active form of learning.
● Study can be followed at the learners' own pace.
● Understanding checks can be built in easily.
● The learning can be followed at the learners' place of work or even at home.
● Time and resources are used effectively.

The disadvantages are few, although they can be serious, and include:

● This type of learning requires a high motivation and commitment by the learner.
● Managerial, trainer or other expert support should be readily available, although this is not always possible.
● Some isolation may be felt by the learner sitting alone in front of a computer screen.
● Some people have an aversion to or a fear of working with computers, although this is a decreasing problem as they became more available and user-friendly.

Learning packages, usually currently on CD ROM, are increasingly available in a wider range of subjects from commercial sources at very reasonable costs, particularly when you consider that the package can be used on more than one occasion. It is also possible to get a custom-written program, either within your organization (if you have an expert computer program writer), or from external professional houses.

Use of the CBT package is relatively simple once the program has been installed on the computer:

1.   The learner is instructed in the operation of the package, although these instructions are frequently an integral and logical part of the program itself.
2.   The learner works through the package at his or her own rate, taking part in the required activities or projects.
3.   If difficulties, misunderstandings or non-understandings arise, reference is made to the supporting manager, trainer or other expert, and/or regular interim reviews are arranged. Up to the present the normal contact has been in writing or on the phone. With the wider availability of the Internet and allied programmes, greater use is being made of computer-controlled fax contact and the e-mail, without the learner leaving the computer.
4.   Learning is reviewed and confirmed at the end of the program, with implementation being contracted on an action plan, agreed with the learner's manager, and the learning put into practice.

Action learning

This approach can be considered a halfway house between formal courses and self-learning as, although it is carried out in a group situation, most of the activity and learning is self-directed and self-controlled. In such cases the 'trainer' is present as a facilitator or provider of resources and help.

The group or set meet regularly, sometimes with, sometimes without the facilitator, and work on the real-life problems of the members, solving these through action research with consequent learning as a result of the action. Or they can set out to learn, as an internally controlled group, some aspect of a common learning need.

A number of variations exist, ranging from the group identifying and solving a common problem, through the group selecting to solve a problem owned by one of their members, to individual members working on their own problems but using the group as a sounding board and support.

The action learning group meet regularly, and as frequently as is agreed by the members. The value of the meetings, in whatever format, is the opportunity for different interpretations, ideas and help to be made available. If they intend to develop some form of instrumentation, the group members use themselves as guinea pigs for questionnaires or tests.

The principal danger can be that the task solution becomes the only objective. How the group members interact, how research is performed and reported, how solutions are proposed and considered and how the final solution is reached are all potential learning areas and must be kept in mind.

Support groups

Action learning need not be as planned as the formal approach described above and learning can take place through what are usually referred to as support groups. These are semi-formal groups of volunteers with similar interests who want to share their knowledge, skills and experience. Frequently these sessions are held during the lunch period, away from the canteen or restaurant, and the members can come from a single part of the organization or be a heterogeneous group from various parts of the company. The meetings, once initiated, can be as regular or irregular, frequent or infrequent, formal or informal, as the members themselves decide. If the members wish, the content of the discussions can extend beyond their own or other work areas to general life situations from which they can learn. Some groups, realizing the benefits of some measure of control, elect chairpersons, often on a rotating basis, and the trainer should always be available for support.

Selecting the appropriate training strategy

With the range and variety of training strategies, approaches and techniques available it can be difficult to select the most suitable or appropriate. Table 8.1 provides a summary and suggests the possible uses.

Table 8.1 Approaches to and uses of training strategies

Learning experience	Possible uses
Action learning – A group or set of people with common aims who meet to take various actions to achieve the resolution of a task and/or learn from each other as they do so	A very practical, self-help group approach as an alternative to formal group or self-learning
Action maze – In an action maze each individual learner is given an information sheet that describes a technical, people or interpersonal problem. At the end of this first piece	Practical group work to develop or reinforce learning or practise skills, attitudes and behaviours

of information, the person is asked to make a decision on the facts available up to that stage

Activity – (or exercise, game, practical or experiential activity). An activity in gathering information, problem solving, task performance, etc

Practical group work to develop or reinforce learning or practise skills, attitudes and behaviours

Brainstorming – Wide-ranging creative discussion to obtain ideas for problem solutions

Creativity. New ideas. Problem solving. Decision making. Group and team training

Buzz groups – Groups of two to six people discussing subject for a short time

Safe environment for expression of views and neutral feedback in group or team without needing to leave the training room

Case studies – Real or manufactured complex problems to be analysed in detail to produce solutions

Group problem solving with application of principles

CAT (Computer-assisted training) – Computer programs inserted or added to other forms of group training

As change of pace and expertise, self-development within groups or on an individual basis

CBT (Computer-based training) – Use of computer programs from software or the Internet to enable, particularly, knowledge learning

Usually for self-development on an individual basis or in work groups linked by an intranet

Demonstrations – Trainer or expert performs an operation, skill or service with learners watching

Practical skill training using real objects or situations to show the operation, etc

Discussions – Subjects are discussed under general control of trainer or elected/selected leader from the group

Promotion of wider understanding and expression of points of view within a group. Use of discussion techniques. Behaviour observation

In-tray or in-basket activity – This is a form of case study that simulates a 'typical' office in-tray with a variety of contents for action. The purpose of the activity is to have the learners sort these items according to learnt criteria and, where necessary, take action

Practical group work to develop or reinforce learning or practise skills, attitudes and behaviours, particularly when the task performer is under time pressure

Table 8.1 *Continued*

Learning experience	Possible uses
Instructional talk/ input session – A trainer presentation of a subject in terms of knowledge, information and details, using a variety of training aids	The basic strategy of a group training event
Lecture – A (usually) uninterrupted talk to a larger audience	Provision of information at conference or symposium
Open learning – (programmed learning, distance learning, learning packages, etc). Text or multi-media packages (audio, video, CD ROM, CD-I, Internet, intranet, etc) with sets of information, questions or tasks	Individual learning, self-development situations. Mixed pace groups. Valuable for regular training-need satisfaction of small number of staff and/or geographically dispersed staff. Stand-alone, with or without support
Projects – An exercise in gathering group information, performing a task or producing material	On- or off-the-job small or larger activities to develop or consolidate and extend learning and encourage cooperative activity
Question and answer – A series of appropriate questions from the trainer to the learning group	To check understanding and encourage interaction and thought at all levels
Reading – from a book, article or handout, in the training situation or away from it	To prepare for learning, to reinforce course or other forms of learning, or as individual self-development
Role plays – Learners given roles, real or artificial, in a group, paired one to one, or in triads, to carry out situation cases	Reinforcement of learning, practising skills, awareness through feedback, attitude change
Seminars – A group of people with similar interests who discuss a group or series of related topics	Updating of knowledge with presentations by subject experts to encourage critical thinking and discussion
Simulations – The duplication of real situations with complex problems, or a game activity with participants taking on roles or positions	Simulation of an activity in problem solving or team development where a real-life case cannot be used directly

Syndicates – Learners form small groups from the full group and meet separately to consider and solve problems, perform tasks, etc. The sub-group views are then presented to the full group

Used in group learning events when it is desirable/necessary to obtain different views or approaches from small groups. Useful for observation of small group behaviour, leadership and membership, and problem solving and decision making

Video (linear) – A video that is shown straight through or stopped at intervals for discussion

Support for other training approaches, change of pace and presentation, expert input, dealing with emotive issues, presenting situations not ordinarily possible on the event

Video (trigger) – A video consisting of short scenarios, after each of which questions are raised for discussion

Guiding discussion on best practices, encouraging discussing and expressing of views, values and ideas. Reinforcing prior learning

9

In-company Training

Surveys suggest that a growing number of organizations are looking to increase their commitment to training at work, rather than sending their staff away to training courses. There is also an increase in interest in having staff initiate and maintain their own learning. The problem is one of identification of needs, of the most effective methods of proceeding and of finding the learning resources. These needs will be better met if they can be guided along the most effective pathway, and this is where the trainer can become involved in a truly supportive role, rather than engaging in a continuous stream of off-the-job training courses.

On-the-job training and self-training approaches

Self-learning has been mentioned in Chapter 8 and the most effective form of this belies its name to some extent – the learner does have a trainer, at least in the background, available for support and advice. In the majority of cases the learner comes to self-learning as a result of advice, guidance and information from the trainer, and this is an area in which you will find yourself engaged more and more in the future.

The following lists the principal on-the-job training approaches, summarizing the methods and commenting on how the trainer can be invaluable in the initiation and support processes:

- GAFO;
- coaching;
- mentoring;
- one-to-one instruction – the 'sitting with Nellie' or desk-training approach;
- team development;

- open learning – audio material, video material, interactive video, comprehensive packages;
- computer-based training.

GAFO

GAFO is an acronym for 'Go Away and Find Out', mentioned in Chapter 1, which can be the simplest form of training at work, although only if done for the right reasons and handled properly. At its crudest, a learner approaches the trainer, or someone who would be expected to have the appropriate knowledge or information, and is constructively told to GAFO. How this is done can, at the lowest level, give the learner the impression that the person is not interested in helping him or her, but applied in an effective manner can help the learner to become non-trainer-dependent. The learning is achieved forcibly with the learner having to seek the answer for him- or herself.

When the information has been obtained the trainer can complete the circle by discussing the results with the learner to explain any points of misunderstanding or lack of clarity. In this way the approach becomes one of guided self-learning.

Coaching

In the majority of cases the trainer does not become involved directly in coaching, as this is a training and development technique used by a manager with his or her own staff when a personal involvement and approach is indicated. The learner follows a training programme while at work, using real work tasks as the vehicles for learning, being supported by the manager and having regular reviews of progress with the manager. In this it differs from most traditional forms of training in the use of actual work rather than the more artificial training course activities.

The trainer can be involved in three ways:

- running training programmes in coaching skills and techniques for line managers who will be involved in these processes;
- running one-to-one or small group training events for staff being coached when the manager or any of his or her staff is unable to provide this expertise;
- advising the coach–manager on the most appropriate methods in individual, specific cases.

The uses of coaching

These can include:

- *Remedial training.* In many cases where training appears necessary, a TNIA (training needs identification and analysis) will demonstrate that, although the learners may have received training in the skills, etc, required to perform their work, this has been forgotten, misinterpreted, or implemented errone-ously, so that the required level of work performance is not being achieved.
- *New or extended duties of work range.* In such cases the individual is required to extend or increase his or her skills beyond the existing situation as a result of having to undertake new work or increase the range of the current work. These increased skills can be achieved by learners attending training courses, but at the expense of resource time and the possible failings of a training course as opposed to learning from real work.
- *Career development.* A skilled and efficient worker may be on the point of promotion or may need job enhancement to stretch his or her abilities and ensure career development or continue job satisfaction. Coaching can offer a very effective method of introducing the learners to these more demanding tasks by their taking on projects that would normally be carried out by their supervisor or manager. This higher-grade work would be delegated to the learners, giving them the authority to carry out the work, but the boss would retain the final responsibility for the results of the task.
- *Training consolidation.* In many cases attendance at a training course is not an end in itself and requires substantial follow-up when the learner returns to work. Training course material is often very general, deliberately so to give a base for a range of situations in which the skills have to be implemented. Back at work, the more general training skill may need to be translated or interpreted to the particular work situation, real-life practice in the skills will certainly be necessary, at-work training in additional parts of the skill might be needed, and so on. If the training is to be made worthwhile in practice the supervisor or manager must accept this continuing need and his or her responsibility to support it, and start coaching projects and assignments to achieve this. Frequently, good training is condemned as having failed when the real cause of the failure is the lack of opportunity, encourage-ment or support to put it into practice.
- *Complete training events.* Coaching might be an alternative to sending learners on expensive training courses, provided sufficient skill exists in the work area to cover the material effectively, particularly when this is linked with real job tasks. The costs and effectiveness of both approaches will have to be considered so that a cost- and value-effective choice can be made. This

approach, of course, can be considered a form of one-to-one, on-the-job instruction when the 'instructor' is either a member of staff or a trainer brought to the workplace to support the coaching/training.

There is no guarantee that coaching, of whatever nature, is less costly than a training course, particularly where several people require the learning; and in some aspects coaching is more expensive in resource time than a course. However, the benefit of the learning taking place at work and the value of real work tasks being undertaken must be significant factors in the cost/value balance. Many learners find that effective coaching has more impact on them than a training course, which they may see as divorced from the working situation.

Benefits of coaching

The benefits of coaching to the individual, the line manager and the organization include:

- improved individual performance;
- improved team performance;
- cumulative improved performance of the organization;
- staff are better informed and aware;
- staff are better equipped for any changes that occur;
- staff are encouraged to be more innovative;
- increased job satisfaction usually results;
- manager eventually has more time for management-level tasks;
- more systematic management progression is possible;
- learning is performed at the workplace;
- there is no need for learners to be away from work and home to attend training courses;
- real work is used, and consequently there is increased credibility in the eyes of the learners;
- the translation from learning to work is eased;
- the coaches themselves develop skills.

Disadvantages

Wherever there are advantages for actions there are almost certainly some disadvantages, real or assumed. Coaching is no exception:

- Time is required for both the learner and coach for the coaching process.
- The organization may not welcome the closer relationships that almost invariably develop between managers and staff.
- The coached skills are not always followed up by opportunities to practise them on a permanent basis.
- Expectations can be falsely raised, for reasons often out of the hands of line managers.
- Some learners see going away on a training course as a bonus (not necessarily a learning bonus!).
- The line manager has to take personal action and be involved in the development of a better relationship with his or her staff – this may be alien to the manager's preferred style of management.
- Excluding some staff, for whatever reason, might damage existing staff relationships.

Mentoring

Mentoring is frequently confused with coaching, but the two are differently defined in training and development of staff. Planning for mentoring involves similar approaches to those for coaching, but on a wider organizational scale. Whereas coaching is usually undertaken by a line manager with staff for operative and similar tasks, mentoring has application at the higher levels and/or more complex situations. Mentoring can be managed in a number of different ways, but the normal approach is for one experienced person (other than the learner's manager, and not usually a trainer) to act, usually over an extended period, as an individual's mentor, supporter, adviser and event arranger.

One example of mentoring might be with a newly appointed management trainee. After more formal induction training, and following or running alongside management training, a departmental line manager or series of managers might be appointed progressively as mentors to the trainee. During the period of mentoring the mentor and learner would have a close association, during which arrangements might be made for the learner to:

- shadow the mentor for a period of time;
- undertake some of the mentor's tasks (under supervision and with coaching);
- complete projects – artificial and real – set up by the mentor;
- attend training events suggested by the mentor;
- discuss a range of relevant topics with the mentor;

- follow a planned programme of visits to various department, either simply as visits or for periods of secondment (under the supervision of the mentor linking with the department head);
- have review and forward planning meetings with the mentor.

The role of the trainer, apart perhaps from acting as mentor for a new entrant to the training role, is in arranging learning events for potential mentors to discuss the most effective methods of mentoring. The trainer may also enter into a discussion about the appointment of the most suitable mentor for particular learners/trainees, especially if they have been offering a widespread programme for potential mentors.

One-to-one instruction (the 'sitting with Nellie' or desk-training approach)

A number of organizations look to one-to-one instruction to develop their employees. This may be either because they are not committed to off-the-job forms of training, do not have the budgets to permit off-the-job training or to employ in-house trainers, are too small to engage in large-scale training (or cannot afford it), or have occupations where it is more effective to train in-house.

The one-to-one approach used to be referred to derogatorily as 'sitting with Nellie' or, more formally, 'training by exposure'. New workers, or those changing jobs, were placed alongside an experienced worker, told to watch what was done, then given their own machine and told to 'get on with it'. This was a very common method at one time, particularly in manufacturing industries such as the clothing trade, where sewing machines were used and it was literally possible for the learner to sit beside 'Nellie'.

The 'Nellie' method has been retained in many areas since those early days, but in a much improved form. This modern approach, generically known as 'one-to-one instruction', can in many cases be more effective than the 'artificiality' of training courses. To ensure that the method is effective, a number of criteria for the instructors must be satisfied. They:

- must be efficient and effective themselves at the task/job in question, because they frequently use demonstration as part of their instruction;
- must have been taught how to instruct rather than being just an experienced worker thrown into the training role;

- must be given the necessary resources to enable the instruction to be performed – two chairs side by side in front of a machine on the production line is far from satisfactory;
- must be allowed sufficient time to prepare for and perform the training;
- must not be expected to maintain personal job output (eg effect on bonus pay systems) at the same time as having the instructor role.

In larger companies a full-time instructor or instructors are found where there is a steady flow of people requiring training/instruction. (The borderline between 'instructor' and 'trainer' in these situations is very vague.) In other situations the instructor is part time and will concentrate much more on the instruction of individuals on an occasional basis. The role of the part-time instructor can be more difficult than that of the full-timer because of the problems of discontinuity.

The cycle of instruction

Following the normal TNIA processes, the cycle of one-to-one instruction can be summarized as:

1. Be fully aware of the apparent training need.
2. Obtain authority to proceed.
3. Identify a person or persons already skilled in the processes to be learnt.
4. Confirm that the person(s) is also skilled in training and one-to-one instruction techniques – if not, it will be necessary to make arrangements for him or her to receive training in these techniques.
5. Analyse the job and/or task and produce a job/task specification.
6. Produce a person specification (again unless already produced in a TNIA).
7. Identify training gap, ie skill required – skill held = training needs.
8. Set specific, comprehensive training objectives.
9. Decide on the most appropriate training/instructional strategy.
10. Design an instructional event or obtain a relevant training package.
11. Produce instruction brief, instructional aids and handouts (or obtain manual).
12. Arrange instruction environment and other administration details.
13. Perform instructional event or issue training package.
14. The learner, within the training area or under the continuous supervision of 'Nellie', is allocated production tasks (preferably in small chunks, if possible) to perform until ready to progress to full production work.
15. Review training and learning.
16. Reassess any instruction or learning needs.

Planning the instruction approach

It is essential that a one-to-one instructor is fully aware and capable of effective methods of instruction, and in this type of training it is essential that the learning steps are clear and in sufficiently small increments for easy understanding. This can be achieved by a detailed step task analysis produced by the instructor prior to the instruction.

Let us consider the task of making a cup of tea. Simple! Boil a kettle of water, pour it into the teapot, allow to brew, pour out the tea, add sugar and milk. But a moment's consideration will suggest that the task analysis is not as simple as this and there are a number of questions to be answered. A fuller analysis could be as follows, the steps being sufficiently detailed for a learner who has never made a cup of tea previously:

1. Unplug electric kettle.
2. Take kettle to the cold tap and remove the lid.
3. Place kettle under the tap, turn on the tap and fill kettle to the required level.
4. Turn off the tap and replace the lid.
5. Return kettle to socket and reinsert plug.
6. Switch on socket (if applicable) and switch on kettle, and while the kettle is coming to the boil:
7. Lay tray with cup, saucer, teaspoon, milk jug (filled with milk), sugar bowl (filled with white or brown sugar, depending on recipient's needs), sugar spoon.
8. Obtain receptacle that holds tea and check availability of measuring scoop.
9. When the kettle boils, take the teapot to the kettle and, having taken off the teapot lid, pour in a little hot water.
10. Swirl hot water around in teapot until it is warm. Pour water out.
11. Replace kettle at socket and replace teapot lid.
12. Bring kettle to boil again.
13. While kettle is boiling a second time, place necessary tea in the teapot, having removed the lid, using measuring scoop – one scoop per person and 'one for the pot'.
14. When kettle boils, take teapot to kettle and fill the teapot to the relevant level.
15. Replace teapot lid.
16. Allow tea to stand in teapot for required time.
17. Place teapot on tray and take tray to person requiring the tea.
18. Either first add milk to cup and pour tea into cup, or pour tea into cup, leaving space for milk, and add milk to taste.

19.   Add sugar to taste from sugar bowl using sugar spoon. Stir tea with teaspoon until sugar has dissolved.

Planning instructional methods

The actual methods of instruction will, of course, depend on the instruction to be given – mechanical operation, desk systems, computer operation, etc – but in the majority of cases a traditional approach should be followed. This is known as the 'Tell, show, do' system referred to earlier.

Example of complex task, eg clerical or computer operation, one-to-one training

1.   The instructor gives the learner a short talk or lecturette describing the (new) procedure, its overall detail and the reason for its introduction. This can be followed by a general discussion between the instructor and the learner.
2.   The manual and/or instruction sheets and any supporting documents can then be given to the learner (who should be allocated sufficient time, not to learn the instructions, but to become familiar with the procedures).
3.   The instructor will have identified the main steps in the procedure and treat these as the staged, divisible learning points. Each stage can then be dealt with in a 'Tell, show, do' manner, moving to the next stage only when the instructor is satisfied with the understanding and skill of the learner.
4.   After each stage the process and the learning should be discussed to ensure that any problems are resolved before moving on to the next stage.
5.   After the final stage the full process and learning are discussed and any remaining problems resolved.
6.   The learner can then be given a task, preferably a real one taken from work, to perform using the new learning. An example of this, for instance, when computer programs are being taught, might be the production on Microsoft Word of a scripted letter or report, in which the grammar and spelling have errors and inconsistencies inserted and the formatting is omitted.
7.   The final action is to discuss the practical session and the learning with the learner, giving feedback on his or her newly acquired skills and confirming any further action necessary.

Instructional events have a duration of from three or four minutes to much longer periods, depending on the complexity of the task. However, all events need to be designed in exactly the same way, with individual differences of scale, and can follow a pattern:

- introduction;
- development;
- consolidation.

The introductory period is self-evident and is essential as a settling–down period, the worst strategy being to launch immediately into the instruction. The learner may be feeling nervous with the environment, the situation, what is to happen and the instructor. Similarly, particularly if the instructor works only infrequently, or part time, there could be nervousness on his or her part.

The development period is when the actual instruction takes place, following the 'Tell, show, do' guideline. Another useful 'rule' is KISS (Keep It Short and Simple). The preferred approach is to use small units of instruction in a natural, sequential order – the teaching or learning key points.

The consolidation stage. On too many occasions instruction finishes with assumptions by the instructor that:

- the instruction method used has been the most effective;
- the instructor has performed in the most effective way;
- the learner has learned as required;
- the objectives have been satisfied;
- the learning is implemented at work.

These assumptions must be tested by simple observation of the learning implementation against the objectives.

Team development

The essence of teamwork is that all the members of the team are working together towards a common goal, each member relating to the others and their roles, respecting each other's abilities and disabilities in their progression towards completion of the task. Teamwork rarely happens without help and support, and the in-house trainer is in an ideal situation to give this, knowing the organization, the team members and, hopefully, having the credibility of being able to help. Team development is not involved only with the team's progress towards completion of the task, but also the development of each member and, where relevant, good interrelationships with other teams in the organization.

The team process was well expressed in a simple model form by John Adair (1986) as shown in Figure 9.1. The basis of the model is that the team process consists of three factors – the task, the group and the individual. Although any team contains these three factors, the team is not effective if the factors are isolated;

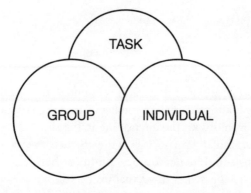

Figure 9.1 The three factors of the interactive team process

rather they should be considered as mutually dependent, interactive and overlapping.

If the team members concentrate on the task alone, the feelings, needs and development of the individuals are ignored and there will be reactions by the members, usually to the detriment of achievement of the task. If the needs of the group receive attention above any other factor the task completion will suffer and the individuals might not all be in tune and not support the group needs and what is being done for them. If the concentration is on the individuals the time spent can jeopardize the achievement of the task and the group may not develop as a complete team. However, if the needs of the task, the group and the individuals are treated in a balanced manner task achievement and human resource progress are much more likely.

A number of concepts and models of team development have been produced over the years, the earliest being with the research of Mayo in the 1920s in the 'Hawthorne Experiment', and later, a classification of the categories of team members – a rather arbitrary classification. These and other research programmes can be used by the trainer in team development, moving from a *forming* stage, through *storming* and *norming* to the end stage of *performing*. This is demonstrated in Figure 9.2.

Each stage is unique and separate and team members exhibit particular behaviours that, if identified and discussed, can help the team to progress through the various stages.

In the *forming* stage, the behaviours exhibited include:

● being formal and polite with each other while wondering internally whether they will be accepted by the rest of the group;

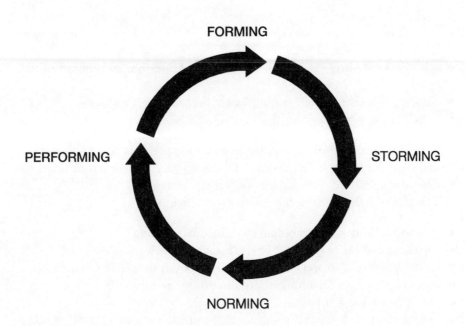

FORMING

PERFORMING

STORMING

NORMING

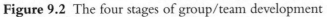

Figure 9.2 The four stages of group/team development

- contributions are rarely contentious or controversial – 'let's not rock the boat';
- keeping contributions to a minimum – 'if I let people get to know me too much, they might not like me';
- avoiding serious contributions – 'they may think I'm an egghead';
- avoiding disclosure;
- not commenting on others' views or giving feedback.

When the group/team members have been together for a little time, and are encouraged to stop being too formal and too retentive of their feelings, the barriers start to come down and the behaviours start to represent the true attitudes of the members – attitudes that can be affected by a wide range of factors not connected with the event, but having an interactive effect. This *storming* stage is when the members are starting to say to themselves: 'I'm not going to sit here like this for the whole event. So here goes. . .'; and in many cases the forming behaviours reverse themselves and the stage is characterized by:

- the expression of strong views;
- challenges made to the views of other members;
- restricted listening to the views of others with increased own contribution;
- resolute, reactive, attacking and defending;

- withdrawal by some members, particularly if they become victims or have their views disagreed with;
- challenges are made by several members for leadership and control of the group;
- challenges to the trainer or team leader become overt and active;
- emotions start to take over from considered behaviour.

If the members are helped to consider their attitudes, behaviours and objectives, progress can be made. If this is successful the cliques and sub-groups start to dissolve and a sense of team identity begins to emerge.

The typical behaviours in the *norming* stage include:

- sharing of leadership according to individual abilities;
- listening and being receptive to the ideas of others;
- active participation and contribution by all, even the quieter members;
- non-participators are brought into discussions and activities;
- an open exchange of ideas;
- any conflict of ideas or proposals are dealt with as win–win rather than win–lose;
- easy self-disclosure;
- looking towards a more methodical way of working with methods agreed by the group.

The positive approach in the *norming* stage, when the team is maturing and realizing the benefits of working together, leads naturally into the final stage, *performing*. This is the mature stage of the team in which there is intense loyalty to the group. This has to be watched carefully as the team can become too closed and fail to improve inter-team relationships. Some of the indicative behaviours for this stage include:

- less dependency on structure and rules;
- individual actions accepted more readily as talents that will help the team;
- high creativity and flexibility;
- openness and trust between the members and the team leader;
- strong relationships and supportive behaviour;
- feelings of 'belonging' to a family;
- individual failing recognized and accepted, and support offered;
- willingness to discuss failings and learn from these as well as successes.

Team development and learning activities can be held both on and off the job, perhaps initially facilitated by the trainer and later handed over completely to the team leader to continue. On-the-job team development utilizes the involvement of the whole team in tasks that not only require real solutions in the course of the team work but can also be used as learning situations, similar to the preferred real-life training in off-the-job group activities.

When the initial stages facilitated by the trainer have been covered successfully the team leader is encouraged and supported in allocating work time for the team to meet and discuss the projects/tasks they have taken part in, their successes or problems, the participation and roles of the team members, any learning that evolved from the tasks, and an action plan for the future. Similar learning discussion events can also be planned to be included at the end of the regular team meetings. A planned pattern of meetings that contains sections such as this can be considered so that the team has the opportunity to meet regularly for purposes other than direct task fulfilment and to give everyone a chance to speak openly about the team and support each other.

More specific training events for the team can be held away from work.

Open learning

Open learning, or distance learning, is the modern equivalent of the old correspondence course and can be a single or multimedia package containing:

- written, hard-copy text, either as continuous text or in a programmed learning format;
- audio material on audio tape;
- video lessons, programmes and presentations;
- interactive video, which is more easily manipulated by the learner than straight video;
- CD ROMs and CD-Is;
- a mixture of the above;
- Internet packages.

All of these approaches can be, and frequently are treated simply as self-learning packages, and the initiator of their use can be the learner's line manager or the training department. The availability of the packages can also be via the training department or directly from commercial organizations. The principal problem that the majority of users of self-learning packages complain about is that it is a lonely way of learning and problems that arise prove difficult to resolve. The best programmes include some form of reference back to the initiator by letter, telephone or e-mail, whereupon an expert can help the learner promptly with resolution of the problem. Use of the packages, however, is made much easier and less traumatic for the learner if there is a local trainer, available in person, on the telephone, via e-mail, or through the organization's intranet. Learners then know they are not alone and that help with problems can normally be given speedily. This means, of course, that the trainer must be fully au fait with the various packages and prepared to help.

In many organizations the training department is responsible for making people aware of the open learning approaches and making them available. The material has multiplied substantially over the past 10 years or so, and both the trainer and the learner must be careful that the quality is sufficiently acceptable to enable learning. This requires an element of planning, and if the training department is introducing open learning packages into training programmes or for straightforward self-learning a number of questions should be asked of the packages under consideration:

- To what extent has the concept of open learning the support of the organization – senior management, line management, training department?
- Which type of open learning package will be the most suitable?
- Is this the best method of learning for this learner?
- How well are the package objectives stated? These should be sufficiently clear for the learners to understand them without difficulty.
- What is the balance between knowledge learning and practical activities? Skill will not be attained from a knowledge-only package.
- Are the activities and tasks pitched at the appropriate level for the learning population?
- What inclusion is there for feedback to learners on the success or otherwise of their practical work? Will it be possible for learners to determine *why* they have gone wrong if this is the case?
- Consider whether the material provided in the package needs to be supplemented in any way. (This may be the addition of more advanced material or material appropriate to the organization and its special needs.)
- Does the material need to be amended in any other way – eg some parts removed or deleted?
- Is the material structured effectively and should it cause only minimal problems?
- What are the licensing arrangements? Is the use of the package restricted to one learner only or is multiple learner use approved – with or without the purchase of a relevant licence? What are the arrangements for copying – a site licence?
- Are the materials up to date and complete for the purpose intended?
- How long does the package need for learning purposes? Is the supplier's statement of this reliable – this can be tested by a dummy run with a non-learner or the trainer personally. Will the required time be (made) available?

- Consequently, planning the introduction of open learning to a learner or group of learners must be performed carefully, considering specific questions relating to the suitability of the learning package itself.

When these questions have been answered satisfactorily, the suitability of the specific package must be considered:

- Do I know about the availability of packages of the nature required? How do I know which package is the most suitable one for this purpose?
- Do I know anybody who has used this package and can evaluate it?
- Has there been a published evaluation of the package and is this valid?
- What arrangement s are there for learner/supplier contact?
- Can the organization produce its own package? Does the organization have people with the necessary additional open learning authoring skills? Has the organization a supply of central experts to respond to learners with problems?

Computer-based training

Probably the biggest 'revolution' in the world of training and development in recent years has been the increased and increasing use of the Internet and intranet to transport training programmes to learners, whether they are individuals or groups within an organization. The logical development of the open learning approach was a learning programme controlled over a network of learners from a central source. This learning material can be in the form of traditional text, e-mail material or electronic Web pages. The learners learn from text pages, follow instructions to perform activities, answer questionnaires and respond to progress questions from the source. They can then take part in subsequent electronic (in e-mail or in an instantaneous 'chat room' format) discussions where necessary, before movement to further parts of the programme.

The more revolutionary techniques, and seen by many people as the way in which electronic methods of learning will proceed, involve the Internet equivalent of traditional methods of training and development. The significant basis of these methods is that any social contact is unnecessary – contact is the interaction of the learner seated in front of the computer monitor with a program that originates with a Web site at any location in the world.

The caveat must be given, as in the case of all 'discrete' forms of training, that any one approach to learning will not suit every learner, and even less cost-effective learning may result if only one method is introduced to the exclusion of the alternatives.

The benefits of CBT

The main benefits offered by CBT include:

Immediacy. The learners do not have to wait for a viable number of participants before a training event can be offered. It is therefore available almost on demand. When a new training demand arises there is often a considerable delay between this – the time taken for the training department to construct an effective training programme, the administration to set up and complement the training event(s), and all the other necessary adjuncts to a live training programme. If the training is available on a computer program, is suitable for learning by this medium and the learners have computers available, the training can be provided almost immediately, which simplifies matters.

Reduction of training time. In most cases training time is reduced. In group training activities the trainer has to pitch the training at a lower level than required by a number (often the greater number) of the participants. This has obvious consequences. If the learner is studying as an individual, using a flexible CBT program, he or she can pace progress to suit his or her own knowledge and skills. This is a common feature of open or self-learning systems and certainly can occur in CBT.

A further advantage, linked to the learner's choice of pace, is that the programme need not necessarily be followed in one session or consecutive sessions. The programme structure may allow it to be taken in sections, at intervals or on a part-time basis. This in itself could help both the learning and the availability of the learner.

Location of training. CBT can be taken to the learner rather than the learners having to come to the training. The traditional approach can cause difficulties of release from work, cost of travelling and accommodation, replacement while the job holder is absent, and so on. The CBT program can even be followed at home, although this requires substantial commitment to learning on the part of the learner.

Consistency. There is a higher degree of consistency than with exposure to live trainers. There are good and bad trainers and many in between: each trainer will present roughly the same material in a different way – some ways will be effective, others less so. Each trainer will have a different level of knowledge that will affect the way he or she puts over the material. If the level is sufficient for the learner, all is well, but otherwise problems can arise. Many trainers have different attitudes and values about the topics for which they are responsible – some may be biased, for example; ideally these are not reflected openly, but this will not always be the case. The CBT program is at least consistent every time it is run – hopefully to 'consistent' we can also add 'correct'.

The disadvantages of CBT

Computer availability. Problems of availability of a suitable computer or even a computer at all have been discussed. This problem is lessening as more and more organizations are installing a wide and sufficient range of computers, and home PCs are similarly increasing in numbers. There may still be problems of this nature for some potential learners, however.

Flexibility. If there is a computer program available for the learning topic it will have only a limited degree of flexibility. This may mean that the learners have to make considerable jumps in relating the material to their own circumstances, especially if other support is not available.

Learning limitations. Not every subject can be learnt from a CBT program. Many, where the basis is the acquisition of knowledge, or knowledge from which skill can develop, are very suitable for CBT application. In general, however, learning areas that have a high degree of human resource interaction are not very suitable. In cases such as this the learning often demands actual interaction under controlled circumstances with a group of other learners – this is not normally associated with CBT. However (and this supports the argument that few training techniques can stand alone) if the CBT program is linked with a short (because of prior learning) training event, where the skills learnt in theory can be put into practice, there can be a successful marriage of techniques. The use of CBT in prior learning for a direct training event not only reduces the length of the event but also helps to ensure that the learners are all at the same learning level. However, the attitude of a training sponsor can be that the learner should/can use only one technique – *either* direct training courses *or* CBT/self-learning.

Inflexibility. You cannot argue with a computer, even though modern programs allow you to interact with it. Most CBT programs are set according to a fixed plan and produce what is, from the program author's point of view, the 'right' answer. In many cases this is fine, but problems can arise for learners if they disagree with the points made in the program or do not understand them. The disadvantages here are the absence of a live peer group with whom to discuss the problems, or the absence of a trainer or expert with whom the problem can be discussed and explained. This disadvantage can, of course, be overcome to some extent if the learner has access, perhaps by phone if not in person, to a trainer, expert or author of the program.

Trainer involvement

Training practitioners and training planners of the 21st century have to accept that there is a CBT application, that this facility is increasing and, whatever the eventual result, they must develop an awareness of what CBT is, what it can and cannot do, and develop skills in applying it to the learners for whom they have a responsibility. In this way the range and success of their clients' learning can be greatly extended and enhanced. The conclusion must be that, for certain purposes and approaches, CBT has a developing part in training and in particular the IT area of training.

In spite of the remoteness and technological aspect of Internet-based learning programs, trainers still have a major part to play. The loneliness of open learning has already been mentioned, and the same comments apply to Internet learning. This is very much the case where the older form of CBT is offered – such programs are equivalent to pages of text in a book, except that they are displayed on screen. More up-to-date and progressive programs are much more interactive, but many people find them too mechanical to make their learning effective. The trainer, acting as an adviser, consultant, support and problem solver, can link with the CBT learner and introduce an effective multimedia approach. Trainers who will be practising in the 21st century must recognize the importance and value of the Internet as a learning medium and ensure their involvement, not just for their own sakes, but also those of the learners.

Planning the use of CBT

The first decision that the trainer must make if CBT is raised as a training consideration is 'Is CBT the most effective format of training for these particular needs, and/or can it (need it) be linked with other learning approaches?' This question, if answered positively, leads to further questions, additional to those detailed earlier when considering the use of open learning:

- Where and what CBT packages are available?
- What type of equipment is required? What standard of equipment is necessary?
- Is this equipment available in the organization or are some purchases necessary?
- What arrangements have to be made for the use of the equipment?
- If the approach is via the Internet, is this available in the organization?
- Are there any restrictions on the use of e-mail in the organization?
- Can the package work efficiently on an intranet or internal network?
- What is the testing pedigree of the package?
- To what extent are supporting materials provided by the supplier or does the learner have to obtain them?
- Are there specific licensing requirements if the package is run on more than one computer?

- Is it possible to try or test out the package before purchase? Are samples available? If not, why not? (Be careful of suppliers who cannot/will not enable this pre-purchase investigation.)

The Web contains an increasingly large number of sites all over the world to which the Internet user can log on. The majority appear to be in the United States, with a smaller number in the UK. Many of these sites are located in universities although an increasing number are being set up by commercial providers.

One of the problems that faces the planner who is considering the use of CBT via the Internet is locating the most suitable source. There is no problem browsing the Web to identify such sites, but which one to use? Years of traditional types of training and development have enabled the build-up of a substantial amount of intelligence about the effectiveness of certain programmes and their providers, but such intelligence is in its early days as far as the Web is concerned. However, more and more organizations are using this facility and it is a reasonably simple task to make contact with these (through, for example, trainer information exchange forums such as UKHRD and, in the United States, TRDEV). The trainers are able to offer first-hand comments on these or in private e-mails and this method is ideal until a universal intelligence is formed.

CBT is not always a better substitute for other forms of training and learning, nor is it necessarily any less expensive – it is frequently more expensive in direct cash terms. The type of learning must be carefully considered as, like any 'prescriptive' form of training, soft skills (such as interviewing) cannot be effectively learnt by CBT. At some time, usually sooner rather than later, personal interventions, with supported learner practice, become essential. Workplace psychology, management and personal commitment can all be factors working against the acceptance of CBT, as they are in many other forms of training, traditional or non-traditional. But CBT, whether through the Internet or by more local methods, is here to stay, has its place in effective self-learning and self-development, and where several learners require a learning approach is a force to be considered.

At the time of writing there are a number of 'camps' with views on the effectiveness and the future of Internet learning – some people doubt the superiority of the computer over other forms of learning help, others see it as far superior, still others see the variety of training provisions of the Internet and other forms of training as an essential mixture in the learning process, and so on. Most of the camps have strong arguments, but the jury is still out.

A number of surveys and research projects are currently being undertaken to try to resolve the question of the value of Internet-based learning packages versus the traditional form of training.

IT Support News, a monthly business publication, has in its June 2000 issue an article by Derek Rice entitled 'Online training'. A copy of the article is included on the organization's Web site, www.itsupportnews.com/june2000/toolbox/toolbox1.htm. In this article, a number of providers and senior management figures in organizations in the United States make their views known.

Some of the sentiments in this article include:

- The online learning segment is growing faster than any other form of learning.
- Online training is less expensive than many other forms of training.
- It's just as good as classroom training and it's about half the price.
- Using technology for learning is at least as good and sometimes more effective than classroom training, especially for hands-on topics such as IT skills.

Then a warning note is sounded:

- It really is dependent on the content. If you just put up page-turning courses. . . employees don't finish the course.
- The company can log on to records and see how much training is being done and by whom.

The article balances the arguments somewhat, by quotes that are not as supportive as the ones above:

- There's an absolute pot-pourri of people throwing stuff out there and calling it e-learning and it's really just e-reading.
- Anyone with a Web site and Internet access can all of a sudden become a training centre.
- Talking with corporations about why they want to migrate to online learning, nine times out of ten it's the money.
- A fallacy is the perception that it releases the need for the employee to take time away from work: 40 hours of learning is 40 hours away from work.
- The reaction from employees has been very mixed about their having to take time in front of their home computer to complete the package.

So far, the consensus is a mixture of the above:

- Training experts think a mix of online and instructor led is still the best.
- Online training brings employees up to speed and levels the start of the classroom training.

● Online training is not ever going to eliminate classroom training, but it can add a lot of value. Instructor-led training will be around forever. . . it has incredible value and always will.

Several research projects are being carried out in the UK, particularly to try to determine the attitudes of employers to the use of Internet training packages compared with other approaches. A recent one – Training Trends 2001 – was carried out by TrainingZone (www.trainingzone.co.uk) and the Training Solutions Show, with 400 training and HR professionals, directors and other managers being asked for information and views on this subject in their organizations. Almost every contact stated that conventional tutor-led training had been held in the previous year and would continue to be used in 2001, some companies increasing their usage.

The proportion of companies using various forms of online training showed a rise from 61 per cent in 2000 to an anticipated 81 per cent in 2001, with coaching and mentoring also showing a significant expansion. Comments on the experience with online training included:

Positive:

Convenient	67%	Flexible	57%
Different	40%	Interesting	34%
Quick	30%	Engaging	14%
Fun	15%		

Negative:

Lonely	37%	Slow	23%
Inflexible	19%	Boring	18%
Fad	10%		

The most emphatically negative part of the report concerned evaluation, particular points being that:

● Only 47% of respondents required their learners to complete an action plan.
● Many professionals are still more intent on collecting 'happy' sheets and 'reactionnaires' than on a more vigorous evaluation of what has been learnt.

On the question of support following the training:

The individual is left to be responsible for implementing his or her   64%
learning

The learner's manager reviews and supports implementation of the learning	35%
The learner's manager offers follow-up	24%
There is a follow-up from the trainer to support the learner	20%
Follow-up? You must be joking	19%

Trainers who are interested in the full comments and research data should visit the sites named.

10

People in Training

People entering the training scene for the first time usually have three major concerns:

1. How about all the training material that I will have to know about and learn? Will I be able to take it all in as quickly as needed?
2. How about all these training techniques and skills that will be needed? Will I be able to learn them and become skilled in them as quickly as needed?
3. Then there are the people who will be attending the courses, etc, I shall be running. Will I be able to cope successfully with them?

The first concern will only be answered by reference to the organization or the training department with which you are to be a trainer. Training can range from purely operational instruction; through supervisory or management skills and specific skills, such as negotiation; to interpersonal and interactive skills concerned with people change. But few trainers are expected to perform this full range, and in any case it is unlikely that early challenges will be excessive.

Most of this book so far has been concerned with the second concern, introducing you to the various skills you will, progressively, need to develop, a learning curve in which your own training will support you.

Many trainers feel the third concern is the most difficult as it impinges on and overlaps the other two, and our general life experience has told us about the vagaries of dealing with people. We may even have gained a reasonable level of success in this and, basically, dealing with people on training programmes is very little different, apart from some special effects owing to the training environment. Training courses in the skills can help, but the best training for coping with people is to deal with them in real life. You will make mistakes – we all have – but learn from them and your training events will become even more enjoyable for both you and your learners.

A number of models can be of help in understanding and coping with people. We shall look at these first, then consider specific types of people who may require different approaches on training events.

Communication

The principal purpose of the trainer with a group of learners is to communicate information, skill performance, etc, to the learners in a manner that actually enables them to change or learn. In practice this is not as simple as that statement! However, a simplistic model of communication suggests the basis of problems that might arise. This is shown in Figure 10.1.

In any communication there is a sender and a receiver and all communication would be effective if these were the only factors. Unfortunately this is not the case. Figure 10.1 demonstrates graphically what happens when a communicator (the trainer) attempts to communicate with a receiver (listener; learner).

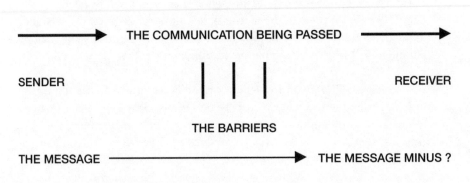

Figure 10.1 A simple communication model

The figure shows that between the sending of the message and its reception there can be a number of barriers. These barriers can be erected by either the sender or the receiver – usually by both, and in the case of one receiver only can vary depending on the different individuals on each occasion. One sender and one receiver can erect certain barriers; another sender and receiver a different set of barriers. And of course one common sender can find different barriers with different receivers, demanding recognition of the barriers in each case. The sender can be the person erecting the barriers and unfortunately may not be aware of these problems.

But a training group has, at the same time, more than one receiver, each of whom can have his or her own particular barriers. The communication model then becomes more like Figure 10.2, with the problems created by many more barriers being exacerbated.

To achieve effective communication you must recognize these barriers – your own barriers and those of the receivers – and do something to avoid them. This process helps to solve any problems you may have had and Chapter 4, in particular, suggests effective approaches by the trainer that will help your message be as

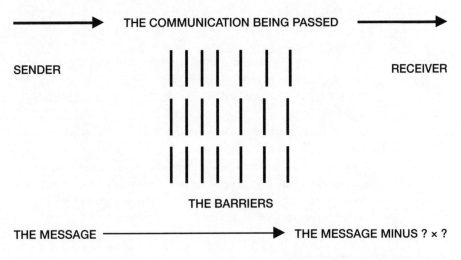

Figure 10.2 A communication model

effective as possible. However, whatever action you may take to avoid problems being caused by your side of the communication model, there will still be various barriers on the receiver side.

Barriers to communication

There are four principal groups of barriers that can be erected when communication is attempted – by you and the receivers:

- language;
- speech;
- psychological effects;
- the environment.

Some are more attributable to the speaking trainer, others to the listening learners.

You, the sender

Language – Appropriate use of vocabulary according to the level of the group. Avoid jargon.

Make clear and unambiguous statements to avoid misunderstanding.

A woolly, rambling approach suggests a woolly mind and the group will soon switch off.

Explain unusual words.

Speech – Remember all the hints in Chapter 5 (eg MERK, the 4Ps, etc). Ensure that you have the highest skills possible as a speaker.

Have a good manner and ensure that your words match your manner.

Use an appropriate attitude – avoid any indication of patronizing the group.

You may be an expert, but don't project as a 'know-it-all'.

Ensure that you have all your subject at your fingertips – prepare!

Your non-verbal communication must be congruent with your verbal communication.

Them, the receivers

Language – Refer to the barriers imposed by the sender; they can all be barriers imposed by the listeners themselves.

Psychological – What inner *pressures* are there on the people with whom you are interacting? These – work, health, domestic, money, earning difficulties, away from home, social pressures – can all have an effect on the listening and learning.

Listeners who are easily affected by *moods* may be in such a mood that listening to you is not a priority.

Forced presence on the course can easily produce a resistance against listening to the trainer, and learning.

Fear produced for any reasons will reduce receptivity although, depending on the reasons and its strength, it can be a strong motivator.

Shyness may have to be overcome by the learner in order to learn, and certainly may be a barrier to learning or clarifying by being unable to ask a question.

Aggression can be the result of forced attendance or feelings against you or the other participants.

Know-it-alls fail to listen as they have 'heard it all before' and 'have nothing to learn here', which can be exacerbated if their presence has been forced.

Too old to learn. This is a common attitude among participants in the older age group, whereas, because of their wealth of experience, they can make the best learners and can be used to support the less experienced in the group.

Status can prevent more junior members from speaking in the presence of their seniors, and vice versa, in case they make fools of themselves or let themselves down.

Environment – *The physical effects* of noise, excessive heat or cold, poor ventilation, restricted space, interruptions and actual work intrusion in the environment can all have their consequences on the extent of listening and learning.

Hopefully, few or none of these effects will be present when you are trying to communicate with the group, but you must be aware of them and be on the lookout for any signals that all is not well.

Maslow's hierarchy of needs

Viewpoints

Different people approach the same situation with different needs and certainly from different viewpoints, and it helps in our training events if, by observation and listening, we can identify our learners' viewpoint. Everybody, most of the time, is experiencing internal dialogues that stem from their particular viewpoints at the time. Figure 10.3 shows a group of people standing on a mountain plateau and suggests the 'viewpoint' internal dialogues they are having.

Translated into the internal dialogues that participants on a training event are having, these suggest what is going on behind the otherwise neutral faces.

For example B, looking all the way round and down and thinking 'Isn't it all wonderful', is taking the global view and in other situations may be uncomfortable if forced to look at specifics before being ready. Interactions with this type of person may need a long introductory period before settling down to the point. However if that 'slowly, slowly' approach is taken with A, who is thinking 'Well, I've reached the top: let's go do something else', the result may be failure. In such a case 'Good morning. Let's get down to business' may be more effective. Why then do people have these different viewpoints?

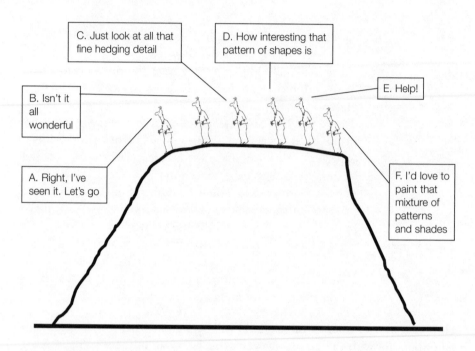

Figure 10.3 Viewpoints

Hierarchy of needs

A hierarchy of needs was produced by Abraham Maslow (1954) who saw that human needs could be identified as being at different levels, the lower levels of which must be satisfied to some extent before the individual can consider the higher levels. This hierarchy can have important implications for the trainer who is trying to encourage a learner or group of learners to apply themselves fully to the learning opportunities. This does not always happen, and in many cases the position of the learner in the hierarchy, perhaps leading to his or her viewpoint, is responsible. The hierarchy is illustrated in Figure 10.4.

The needs are intrinsic to human nature and at the lowest level represent the need to survive physically and physiologically – the requirement for air, food, water and sleep. These are essential for life and must be present before the next level, that of the more long-term survival factors – shelter, clothing, a job, job security, and so on. These appear basic to all of us, but without these survival factors the individual has no motivation to try to move further up the hierarchy and little that anyone can do will produce movement.

When the two lower levels of basic physical needs are satisfied the scene is set to allow deeper desires to surface and involve the more emotional needs.

Such factors as belonging (to society, to a group, to a family), friendship and affection and embracing the involvement of other people will normally be the next satisfactions for humans to aim at. Of course, there are individuals to whom these needs appear to mean nothing – the loner, the hermit, the recluse – but even to them belonging is part of their existence: would the loner be content if no other people existed?!

At the next stage of the hierarchy is a deeper psychological level that involves the need for an individual's esteem, in terms of both self-respect and the respect of others, competence, independence, self-confidence and prestige. The person's attitudes and motivation to perform, including learning, interacting with others and behaving in an appropriate way with others, have now reached an outward-looking concept of life, rather than the egocentric, inward-looking attitude that restrains upward movement.

Once this important level is attained and the individual is in effect at peace with him- or herself the aim can be self-actualization, in which self-fulfilment in the widest way, real self-expression and creativity can be achieved. The individual's work may or may not offer these outlets, but if not they will be sought away from work. The painters, writers, sculptors, top sportspeople and entrepreneurs have achieved this level, often moving to these expressive areas from more mundane jobs where the earlier hierarchical needs were achieved. Self-actualization is self-perpetuating and produces a dissatisfaction with successive achievement. The artist who has produced a painting strives to produce a better one; the writer who has created a literary work will not rest until an even better work has been completed; the entrepreneurial businessman who has built up a successful enterprise will then seek other avenues for business success, often without the desire to make even more money.

The practical point of the model is that there is little point in attempting to motivate someone to achieve a particular level when the level at which they find themselves has not been successfully conquered.

The Johari Window

People will come to your training events not only with different levels of skills but also significant differences in their behaviour and self-knowledge. A model known as the *Johari Window* can be used both to help people to identify where they are and to enable the training to try to help them improve their situation.

The model originated with Joseph Luft and Harry Ingram – hence the title, which is composed from their forenames, Jo + Harry (Hari). The model raises the concept that there is a four-paned window (as shown in Figure 10.5) that can be seen through to show the various aspects of people's behaviour. If these

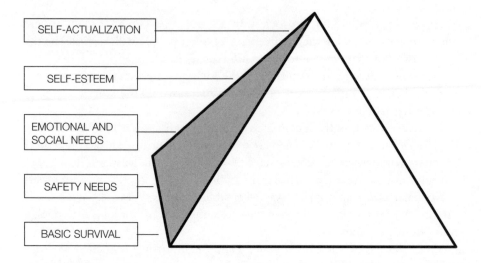

Figure 10.4 Maslow's hierarchy of needs

	Known to self	Unknown to self
Known to others	ARENA	BLIND SPOT
Unknown to others	FAÇADE	UNKNOWN

Figure 10.5 The Johari Window

aspects can be recognized we can adjust our dealings with people accordingly or, in a training environment, awareness can be increased to enable people to modify their behaviour. The Window is two-way, with information flowing out from people and feedback from others entering the individual Window.

Each pane in the Window represents knowledge at the various levels. The panes will not be equal sizes from one individual to another, and each individual's Window is capable of modification, either as an increase of trust between people or as a result of accepted feedback interchanged between individuals.

The top left pane is entitled the Arena and represents what we know about ourselves and is also known by others – the area of open and public knowledge. The size of this pane varies considerably according to the openness of the individuals and their willingness to expose information about themselves. This pane is very much under the control of the individual, and even with feedback the overt image is determined completely by that person.

Another pane, related to the Arena and capable of modification in a similar way, is the Façade or Hidden area. This section of the awareness model is concerned with things that are known about oneself, as with the Arena, but unknown to others. The Façade is clearly related to the various public acts or roles we perform, roles we want other people to consider as the 'real' us.

Our acting ability determines whether the Façade is maintained or whether our act is discerned and the pane is transferred into the Arena. Many people maintain a Façade to deliberately mislead others because it gives them a false sense of security or because they are very 'private' people. At worst they may mislead for some nefarious purpose. Other individuals may be afraid that if they reveal their true selves they will suffer emotionally.

The third pane, the Blind Spot, represents the area about us of which we are unaware, but that is observable to others. This pane can be reduced and our awareness of ourselves increased as a result of growing trust with others. In such cases feedback can be given and accepted and behaviour modification considered. The more the feedback the greater the reduction possible in the size of the Blind Spot.

The final Window pane is the most difficult as far as awareness and behaviour movement is concerned, for this is the Unknown area and it contains information about ourselves of which neither we nor others are aware. Some of these aspects may be so deeply hidden that they never surface, but others may be lurking just underneath the psychological surface, and with the right stimulus may come to light. Such Unknown aspects may be skills that have never emerged, or which may require significant pressure, trauma or solicitation to bring them out.

The format of an individual's Window can determine his or her skills in their interactions with others, and a person's awareness skills will enable him or her to assess others. It is obviously difficult to assess the values of somebody's Window in a short period of time, particularly if the person has a strong Façade and is skilled at protecting this; the longer the interaction the more change can occur in the Window with consequent help in improving interaction. The Façade will rarely completely disappear, since few of us will divulge everything about ourselves to everybody, but 'poses' can be reduced when trust increases. If all the three active panes of the Window that can be affected – Arena, Façade and Blind Spot – are reduced to a realistic minimum there is every chance that the Unknown area will be reduced, with other skills coming to light.

It is difficult to identify certain individuals, such as one with a small Arena and large Façade. These are usually shy or very quiet people with whom it is difficult to have an interaction. Little movement will occur and interactions will continue to be difficult if their Window is not modified. One result of their Johari profile is that they will almost certainly have a large Blind Spot, because they are not given or do not accept feedback, and a large Unknown area, as this is not encouraged to open. They will rarely seek help and, in a more formal interaction, the leading person will have difficulties communicating and assessing not only where the problems lie but whether the advice or support offered is being accepted.

Neuro-linguistic Programming (NLP)

NLP has appeared only relatively recently on the training and development scene, and stems mainly from the work in the 1970s of John Grinder and Richard Bandler (1979). It is a complex concept, principally because it is essentially an aggregation of almost all of the skills required in dealing with people. NLP has gathered the many facets of interactive and other skills together into a cohesive model concerned with responding effectively to other people, and understanding and respecting their views, opinions and needs – people skills.

Because NLP has its roots in psychotherapy the language used can be daunting and attitudes to the approach range from excitement and a sense of evangelism, through scepticism of its ability to transfer from therapy to training and its effectiveness as a technique, to horror and rejection. Many of its strongest proponents see it as a panacea for all training and development needs, and there may be some truth in this – not because of NLP itself but because it encompasses all the best practices for dealing effectively with people. Others, the strongest sceptics, see it as a 'flavour of the month', something that has occurred on a number of occasions in the field of training and development. But one important aspect of the NLP concept (one with which few can disagree) is that people skills are anchored in communication, and effective communication can only be measured by the response you receive.

Some aspects of NLP

Some of the aspects of NLP that have a direct relevance to and use in training and development include:

- *Matching* – As the name suggests, this is matching the tone and tempo of your voice and your breathing rate to that of the person to whom you are speaking. If he or she speaks softly, so do you; if he or she speeds up, so do you, but always without obvious mimicking, aping or being too extreme in your matching. The model suggests that this matching will subconsciously flatter the other person who will see and accept you as being in tune with them.
- *Mirroring* – This has been recognized as an effective approach of non-verbal communication for a long time. It involves a deliberate mirroring of the other's posture, attitude and body language, sometimes unconsciously. If it is done consciously we improve our chances of establishing rapport.

  Examples of this mirroring include sitting forward when the other person does so; mirroring the movement 'tells' that person that you recognize the importance of what he or she is saying and are willing to listen and consider. Smiling is something we frequently do when another person smiles at use, but again a deliberate action can have the desired effect. Many other forms of mirroring – for example folding your arms when another does so – have to be done carefully and subtly so that the other person does not get the impression that you are mocking, but performed carefully the other person's subconscious will recognize and react to the empathic action.
- *Pacing and leading* – This refers to recognizing and respecting the emotional state or feeling of another person. For example, if the other person is demonstrating anger, pacing does not involve being angry in turn but demonstrating that you recognize the anger and see the reason for it. If the reason for the anger is justifiable you can also show support and the desire to care for and help them. Again the intention of these actions is to establish a rapport that will help the interaction to proceed smoothly and effectively, in most cases the pacing changing to a leading of the other person into a more acceptable state.
- *Eye cues* – Known in NLP as VAK (visual, auditory and kinaesthetic responses), these are, in many ways, an extension of standard non-verbal eye signals, but NLP suggests that specific eye movements will tell an observer how the other person is thinking during the communication. One possible snag in observing these effects has been found by a number of people, as it involves looking very directly at the eyes of the other person. This can be a difficult way of communicating for many and can involve them in embarrassing situations!

Although the eye clues are not universal in application they suggest that when right-handed people move their eyes in the direction of the arrows they are:

Imagining an image

Remembering an image

Constructing sounds

Remembering sounds

Having feelings and internal emotions

Having an internal dialogue

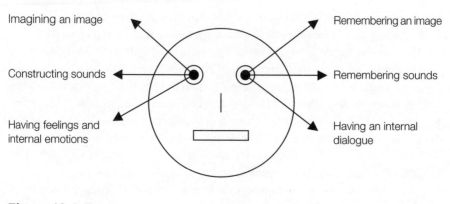

Figure 10.6 Eye cues

If the person is looking straight forward, but in an unfocused way, visual images are being created or remembered.

- *Calibration* – This is claimed by NLP to be the key to effective communication and is described as the reading of other people, their eye and facial movements, breathing and other forms of non-verbal signals. Using all the available signals you can try to assess the feelings of the other person and how effective your inter-communication is. There are no rules by which you can be guided as every interaction will be different, just as people are different, and you will need to use all your skills of people observation to pick up the signals that will enable you to calibrate the interaction.

The competence ladder

The task and technique skills you will learn, and the skills of coping with people, all add up to your total skills as a trainer with the objective of helping people to learn and change their knowledge, skills and attitudes to a more effective level. This does not happen immediately, and every learner, including you, goes through various stages that can be described as the 'competence ladder', as shown in Figure 10.7.

Unconscious incompetence. Many of us carry out our actions without considering how effective we really are and frequently wonder at a superficial

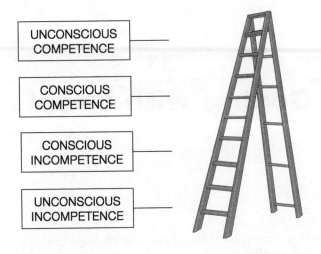

Figure 10.7 The competence ladder

level why things do not always work out as they should. The common reason for this is that we are not very competent, but we are unaware of this incompetence.

Conscious incompetence. Something may happen that lets us know that we are not as competent as we thought (or didn't think) we were. This might have been a serious self-inspection of our interactions and their results; or we may have received critical feedback about our skills; or, for whatever reason, we attended a training event that helped us identify the level of our skills. As a result we move up the ladder to awareness of our incompetence.

Conscious competence. This comes about as a result of our actions to improve and practise these skills, taking care to keep in mind all the techniques and approaches we should be using. Practice is an important aspect of this stage, during which we are deliberately trying to improve.

Unconscious competence. The ultimate level reached after considerable practice, both in a training situation and in real life, in which skills become second nature. The parallel is with learning to drive a car, in which during the learning stage we consciously think about changing gear, depressing pedals, steering as required, and so on. After passing the test and developing experience through a significant amount of driving we begin to realize that we have changed gear, braked, corrected steering, etc, without thinking about what we were doing.

11

Coping with People

Chapter 10 was concerned with various models relating to the people with whom you will come into contact during your training, and some comments on why they behave as they do. You will hear many scary stories from seasoned trainers about their experiences with people – some of them are true, and I could recount a number of my own! But major problems with people on courses are not too frequent, and many of these could usually have been avoided by a closer observation of behaviours exhibited and the ways incidents occur. The vast majority of people attending training programmes do so because they want to learn, and consequently will work with the trainer to achieve this; but there will always be a small number who can be described as difficult participants, usually because they have one or more of the barriers described in Chapter 10. But what do you do when you encounter a 'difficult' participant and you have no immediate clues as to their motives. It would be simple to say, 'Do the best you can', but there is more guidance available than this!

Handling difficult replies to your questions

Many of the problems occur as a result of your asking a question of an individual or the group during a training event. Posing questions in an effective manner has been discussed earlier and if you have practised this you can expect a response more or less in the form you anticipated or hoped for. But not all responses will fall into these categories and you must be prepared to deal effectively with these. Often, when planning the questions that you will be asking during a session, it will be possible to identify the occasions when the responses will be less than you hoped for. These can include:

When the answer is incorrect or incomplete. Whatever you do, do not ridicule or ignore the answer, or be sarcastic about it – it may have been given in good faith. Acknowledge the response and also any part that is correct. Then move on to the remainder and either correct it or, preferably, probe the responder, or perhaps the remainder of the group, for the correct answer.

When the answer is woolly, but the responder obviously had the correct answer in mind. Comment that you believe that you understand what the responder is saying, but it would help you if he or she could clarify their answer – if necessary, select the parts of the response that were woolly.

When your question is received with silence. Ask yourself 'Was the question relevant?', 'Was the question clear and understandable?', 'Have I overestimated the possible responders' ability?', 'Am I sure we have covered that area?' (It may, unusually, be that you have upset the group to the extent that they don't want to answer you!!)

The silence may be accompanied by puzzled looks – clear indications that the question has not been understood, rather than any other reason. So rephrase it in a clearer manner or, in the case of a complex question, break it into smaller steps.

When the response asks for your views. This can be a ploy used by some members of a group, the reason being either to put you on the spot or, more reasonably, to avoid having to commit themselves.

What are difficult people?

Any trainer running a training course or workshop will encounter what appear to be problem people. The resulting problems can cover a wide range of situations and part of the trainer's responsibilities is to deal with them in an effective manner, otherwise there is the danger of their escalation and of the problem people contaminating others in the group. In the generally difficult area of training and development for people skills, coping with these people is probably the hardest. You will find many suggestions for this and many of them will work *in a number of cases*. People differ considerably and an approach that worked with one person is not guaranteed to work with another.

Two particular aspects of dealing with difficult people need to be considered before starting any remedial action or even considering whether to do anything and you are advised to spend some time thinking about them:

- Few feel that they are as difficult as they appear to be – the majority of these 'difficult' people are normal people reacting negatively to difficult or unsatisfactory *situations*. Consequently if the situation is corrected the difficult person ceases to behave in this way. Of course there are people who are inherently difficult because of personality factors, but: a) we encounter few of these, and b) very little can be done about these under normal circumstances.

- The criterion that must be kept in mind when considering the difficult behaviour of others is first to look at our own behaviour. Have we done anything to produce the other's reaction? One significant fact when dealing with people is that *behaviour breeds behaviour* – has anything that we have done contributed to this person's behaviour?

Pre-action considerations

When you have a difficult person or situation with whom/which to deal, a useful exercise is to sit down and quietly consider as many aspects as possible. The following list gives some guidance on the areas for consideration.

- **What is the problem?** Define what is happening and the effect and the extent of the effect it is having on: a) you, b) others, c) the work. Many problems, when considered in a logical and analytical way, frequently turn out not to be problems at all or 'problems' about which it is not worth taking any action.
- **What are the symptoms?** In as much detail as possible, describe how the problem is demonstrated:
  - What is being done that is not acceptable?
  - What is *not* being done that should be?
  - Who is responsible for these actions? Only one person? A number of people? Are you included?
  - When is the action being, or not being, taken? Is there a behaviour trigger you can identify?
  - How did the information come to light?
  - How is the error evident? What effects does it have?
  - How often does the error occur?
  - Where does the error occur? Does it have effects in other areas?
- **Possible causes.** Why do you think, on the evidence you have at the moment, the errors or omissions occur? Consider as many possible causes as you can, but be careful not to come to any conclusion at this stage.
- **Is it my behaviour or that of others?** Is there anything I can identify that I or others have done (or not done) that has contributed to the problem? Detail what these factors are or may be:
  - Has any inappropriate behaviour taken place that has caused the other's attitude and behaviour?

- Have the needs of the 'problem' person been addressed or met – training, progression, development, post-training support, etc?
- To what extent has there been communication between the person and me or with others that might have some bearing on the problem?
- Is it possible to identify an event or period in which the problem started and that might be identified with inappropriate behavioural activities? Was the person turned down for something in an inappropriate manner? Were proposed ideas ignored or rejected out of hand?

- **Action.** What action should I now take to resolve this situation? The decision may be to take no action, to change specific parameters, to interview others, to interview the problem person. Whichever action is decided, detailed planning for it must take place.
- **Obstructions.** Are there any particular problems or obstructions I can identify that will interfere with or make difficult the carrying-out of the proposed action? How can I overcome these?

There may be situations you encounter in which it is unavoidable that drastic disciplinary action be taken. As the trainer you do not usually have the authority for this action, so your first recourse must be to your training manager, with as much 'evidence' as you have of the problem. The next stage is usually for the learner's line manager to be contacted and informed of the problem – this may result in the learner having to be sent back to work. Do not feel guilty about this (provided you did everything feasible to resolve the situation) as the rest of the group would almost certainly have been affected negatively if the problem person had stayed. Such disciplinary action would cover, obviously, drunkenness during the course day, unacceptable behaviour in the course accommodation, or with other participants, and flagrant breach of regulations.

Behaviour

Behaviour has already been mentioned several times and in dealing with problem people, as in all people interactions, behaviour is the core of the problem – that of the person, your own, of others or all of these. The criterion stated earlier must always be remembered – except in rare cases, behaviour will breed behaviour. Treat people in a humane, gentle, caring manner and there is a much greater likelihood that they will respond in an open way. Treat them coldly, formally, and their responses are likely to be uninformative, curt and unfriendly. If someone comes to you bristling with anger and you respond in a like manner the anger will spiral and reach a stage when the 'interaction' will fail; do not react to the anger, whatever the provocation, and gradually the other person will start to cool down and be more amenable to discussion.

Consequently the behavioural temperature of the interaction might be influenced by your behaviour and you will have to make a positive decision about this; not only what you are going to say but also how you are going to say it, and also ensuring that your verbal and non-verbal behaviours are congruent. But understand that you will not always succeed, usually for reasons beyond your control.

First steps in handling situations

There are many areas of difficult behaviour that might be encountered during a training event. These are some of the major ones:

Anger, insolence, shouting
Cynicism
Dominance
Fleeing and non-involvement
Inappropriate laughter
Inattention
Interrupting
Intolerance or copping out
Irrelevance or red herrings
'Let me tell you what happened to me'
Racism, sexism, etc
Silence
Speaking uninvited for others, and dominance
The 'joker'
Falling asleep

Remember that the first step in handling a difficult person situation is dealing with it as soon as it starts to happen – there could have been earlier instances that you may not have noticed, or when you avoided taking any action. It is obviously difficult to forecast what may or may not escalate, but certainly if two similar events occur, even minor ones, with the same person, take these as warning signals and do something about the situation, or at least be prepared to take action on a further occurrence.

Each of these behavioural areas of difficulty requires a rather different approach to resolve, and, as noted earlier, the same approach for what appears to be the same problem may have to be modified for different people.

Problem behaviour	Possible solution approach

Anger, insolence, shouting

These are all very aggressive behaviours that must not be allowed to continue, as they risk disrupting the training event. In the case of anger and shouting (whether at the trainer or a fellow learner) there must have been a trigger. The trainer should be (have been) aware of the reasons and should take whatever steps are necessary to resolve them and cool the aggression. Open insolence cannot be tolerated and positive, even disciplinary action via the training manager must be taken to resolve the situation.

Fleeing and non-involvement

Be aware of apparent non-involvement – in so many cases it is not real non-involvement. The individuals who appear to be opting out may be listening intently, but are too quiet or too shy to speak out in the group – this is particularly the case in the early stages of a course. If the course includes a lot of experiential activities remember that in some cultures the norm has been the traditional approach to training (sit and listen!) and participants may be wary or unsure of being asked to open themselves and take full part in the activities.

- ***Do not*** *'name the victim' by asking the quiet person a direct question, trying to force an answer. By all means try to bring the person in. After someone has made a contribution and if the quiet person is known to be experienced in the topic, reference can be made by asking what (not if) he or she has anything to add from their experience.*
- *If the group or several are quiet in this manner, when activities are introduced make some comments about contributions and learning, and make the groups small – even very shy people are more likely to speak up in a small group than in the full group.*
- *Start activities with ones that are not too challenging and also ones where the group can nominate a reporter for the group when they return*

to the full group. (I would be the last to suggest asking another member to propose the quiet one!)

— *When you want answers from the group, and you know one or two will not speak voluntarily, ask the question in a round-robin, creeping death or Russian roulette approach of everybody in the group.*

— *If there are several quiet members and you are going to have paired activities, pair the quiet ones together. Some people suggest a quiet one with a non-quiet one, but I feel that this holds too many dangers of stultifying the quiet member.*

— *Encourage the group themselves to bring in the quiet members, perhaps in a discussion or other activity, telling the group that they will need to obtain the views of all the members.*

Inappropriate laughter

If there is laughter in the group and you are not saying anything remotely humorous ask yourself why there is laughter. As in so many cases, start with yourself – are you unconsciously saying something that would cause laughter at you? Have you used the wrong word, or given incorrect information, has your zip worked loose, etc?

— *If you cannot identify anything as causing the laughter, ask the people involved if they have something amusing (whatever it might be) to share with you and the rest of the group.*

Inattention

This is similar to intolerance (see below) and the first stage is self-questioning about your own actions. There could also be a problem with an individual's or individuals' ability to listen as opposed to doing something. Have you talked longer than the normal attention span? (In a session this is approximately 15–20 minutes without the introduction of some change.) Otherwise the intolerance actions can be carried out to identify and resolve the problem.

However, inattention may not be the real case. The apparent problem is usually demonstrated by a very 'laid-back' attitude including physical 'lying back' in the chair, and/or a bored look. This may be the relaxed attitude of the person who in fact is taking everything in (but is he or she contributing when the group views are sought?).

— *A 'safe' method is to have a word during a break and ask whether the course is giving the individual what is wanted/expected, how he or she feels about it, etc. Suggest that the individual might get more out of the course by participating more frequently as you are sure he or she has valuable views to offer.*

— *If, when you approach the individual, the responses are very guarded or even negative, raise the question of what might be done to help him or her learn. Of course, even if you receive a very sensible response, time on the course may not permit any action, so you would then have make some other arrangements.*

Interrupting

This is linked with the behaviour category of 'shutting out', which is a specific activity to exclude others (particularly those who are speaking). The more this is allowed to continue the more it escalates and disturbs the group action.

— *Discuss with the group the effects of interruption.*

— *As soon as the interrupter stops speaking return the discussion to the original speaker.*

— *If there is a habitual interrupter who will not stop, have a word after a session and discuss the effect the behaviour is having on the less powerful and the more powerful members of the group.*

Intolerance, cynicism

When individuals or groups are intolerant of the training or the trainer, or are sitting there thinking 'What a load of rubbish this is – what am I doing here!', the visual evidence, apart from the vocal comments to this effect, includes rolling eyes, smirking, side-talking, looking bored and yawning frequently.

— *Ask yourself whether this reaction is due to your actions or inactions. Are you being boring, repetitive, or simply talking too much about matters that are of no relevance to the group?*

— Raise the question openly by means of interim validation of how the group feel the session/course is going. This can be done by using an interim validation diagram — a questionnaire such as a thermometer on which they are asked to note where they feel the 'temperature' of the session is, a 'speedometer' asking whether they think it is going too fast or too slowly, blob reviews, three words/phrases or similar approaches.

— If the signs are being exhibited by an individual and it is starting to affect the group, raise his or her apparent intolerance or boredom directly with him or her.

Irrelevance

This is frequently linked with red herring contributions and usually occurs with people who either cannot understand the material that is being presented or simply like to hear the sound of their own voice. If the former case is suspected a validating activity is suggested to confirm whether everybody understands to that stage. The latter case is more difficult to control and some approaches include:

— Thank the contributor for the comment, however irrelevant, then immediately pass a question to another member whom you know has something relevant to contribute.

— If the member continues with irrelevancies or red herrings in spite of your attempt to divert, when he or she has made one of these contributions comment on what has been said and ask either: a) that person how they see his or her point as relevant to the topic, or b) the group whether they wish to look at these points (or go back to the main topic).

— Generally remind the group, without any indication of criticism, of the objectives of the session and the limited time available to achieve these.

'Let me tell you what happened to me'

This, or something similar, is the entrée statement of the inveterate teller of anecdotes 'from their experience'. Real-life stories can help a session along, but only if they are relevant and do not crop up too frequently, as they can do with this type of person.

- *If the 'short' anecdote, particularly when this occurs on several occasions during a session, starts to become a full and lengthy story, interrupt and ask the speaker if he or she can either summarize it as time in the session is running short, or simply say that there isn't time – so he or she can retain the story until the break.*

Racism, sexism, etc

These, and the other 'ism' areas, are not acceptable in statements in a public arena, eg a training group, as apart from being generally insulting they may attack people in the training group. The result could be an aggressive situation that will destroy the flow of the training. This is not to say that they should be taboo subjects, but the trainer must ensure that they are dealt with delicately.

Silence

Comments have been made on this problem in relation to questioning. But if the group are silent generally consider whether they are performing some activity (breaking the silence would cause real problems), or are they doing nothing when they should be? Other reasons may include shyness, embarrassment, avoidance or withdrawal, or even non-cooperation or actual resistance to you or other members.

- *Comment to the group on what you are observing and ask whether there is a problem.*
- *Confront the individual with the issue.*
- *Encourage them verbally or non-verbally.*
- *Use questions, even closed ones.*
- *Modify what is happening to ease the situation – will an icebreaker or other exercise help or hinder?*

Speaking uninvited for others, dominance

When you ask a question generally to the group it is acceptable for anybody to respond. But if you direct the question at a particular person, usually naming him or her, and someone else answers before he or she has a chance, this is not acceptable behaviour. Frequently the person who does this is the one who, when a question is aimed at the whole group, always comes in first with a contribution. This can reach such extremes that the rest of the group simply stop answering.

- *Even if the uninvited person makes a response, always go back to the person at whom the question was aimed, and ask again for his or her views, having recognized the uninvited response.*
- *For the constant responder, again recognize the contribution, but immediately turn to the rest of the group to obtain other views.*
- *Members who take over the contributions in this way are usually ones in the group who make every effort to be dominant. Continued reference to the rest of the group, however difficult it often becomes, must be continued, otherwise the individual will consider that he or she is being allowed to dominate.*

The 'joker'

There will usually be members of a training group who are natural wits. They help to keep the group alive and help you in your task, acting frequently as a counterbalance (without upsetting the balance) to the heavier training material or discussion activities.

- *Learn to identify the appropriate and inappropriate forms of humour and quietly encourage the former, but controlling it so that it is kept within bounds.*

There can, however, also be members who cannot seem to open their mouths without trying to be witty and making the group laugh.

- *This latter case is inappropriate behaviour and is disruptive to the group. In fact, after laughing on the first few occasions the laughter diminishes, ceases and changes into antagonism against the joker, unless you put a stop to it. The reason behind this behaviour is usually a nervous form of avoiding expressing real feelings. Try to get the joker to express his or her feelings, opinions, views and so on, without the wisecracks. But if the behaviour continues, you must point out to the individual the extent to which his or her behaviour is affecting you*

> *and possibly the group. A private talk during a break to help the individual disclose his or her concerns might help to sort out the situation.*

And finally, the ultimate:

Falling asleep
Do not jump to the immediate conclusion that your presentations are so boring as to put people to sleep. There can be a wide range of reasons – physical or medical – why the person has felt the need to nod off. The first thing you have to ensure is that he or she is only asleep – other reasons for apparent sleep, although rare, are not unknown.

– *Try not to embarrass the person or, even worse, make him or her wake up with a start. One possible method is to stop talking and create a silence, then start talking again at a higher volume. Otherwise, enlist the help of the person's neighbour to quietly and sensitively waken him or her – there will be much less embarrassment if someone other than you does it.*

– *Check whether there is sufficient ventilation in the room and ensure that lunch is not a heavy meal. The first session after lunch is usually referred to as the 'pudding session', since, if the meal has been heavy, the group can sit there in a very somnolent attitude. DO NOT try a talk – this is almost a certain way of sending them to sleep. Use an activity, preferably a physical one, until the sparkle comes back in their eyes.*

The comments above do not represent all the 'difficult' types of learner you *might* encounter over a period of time of training – I have been in the profession for some time now and I have certainly met them all! But they are not so common and you may be lucky in your encounters. Remember that the vast majority of participants of a training event are there to learn, want to learn, look to you to help them to learn and also to remove any distractions that will stop them in this process. In most training events you will find pleasant, friendly, helpful, cooperative participants and, if you are doing your job effectively, both you and they will enjoy the experience. But consider the converse situation – the course is running like clockwork (so did the last one and, forecasting, so will the next ones) – when you have a little experience under your belt, aren't some hiccups in the form of people challenges likely to make the event more active and interesting? (As long as it doesn't escalate to the point of destroying the event!)

Conclusion

If you become completely au fait with the subjects you are going to present; are aware, progressively, of the wide range of techniques, approaches and skills and become able to practise them; develop a strong awareness of people, their verbal and non-verbal behaviours and barriers; and develop the skills of coping with difficult situations – whether caused by people or the environment – then you are a professional trainer. This will take an indeterminate period of time, but hopefully you will be supported by your training manager and your peers, and it will happen. There are many trainers around now and in the past who have 'qualified' to this level without being 'superpeople'. Having achieved this status you will be enjoying training to such an extent that you may wonder what other people see in their jobs! And, even more important, the people with whom you interact, in whichever of the many ways of training, will be learning their skills as a result of your interventions.

References and Recommended Reading

Activities

Elgood, Chris (1996) *Using Management Games,* 2nd edn, Gower
Jones, Ken (1997) *Games and Simulations Made Easy,* Kogan Page
Ments, Morry van (1999) *The Effective Use of Role Play,* 2nd edn, Kogan Page
Rae, Leslie (1999) *Using Activities in Training and Development,* 2nd edn, Kogan Page

Coaching, etc

Atherton, Tony (1999) *How to be Better at Delegation and Coaching,* Kogan Page
Parsloe, Eric and Wray, Monika (2000) *Coaching and Mentoring,* Kogan Page

Computer, Internet and Web training

Crainer, S (1995) *The Complete Computer Trainer,* McGraw-Hill
Duggleby, Julia (2000) *How to Be an Online Tutor,* Gower
Greer, T (1998) *Understanding Intranets,* Microsoft Press
McConnell, D (2000) *Implementing Computer-supported Cooperative Learning,* 2nd edn, Kogan Page
McDowell, Steve and Race, Phil (1998) *500 Computing Tips for Trainers,* Kogan Page
Steed, Colin (1999) *Web-based Training,* Gower

General training techniques

Adair, John (1986) *Effective Teambuilding,* Gower

Bailey, Diane (1998 et seq) *The Training Handbook,* Gee (also on CD ROM with updates in this form)

Bandler, Richard and Grinder, John (1979) *Frogs into Princes,* Real People Press

Bourner, Tom, Martin, Vivien and Race, Phil (1993) *Workshops that Work: 100 ideas to make your training events more effective,* McGraw-Hill

Buckley, Roger and Caple, Jim (2000) *The Theory and Practice of Training,* 4th edn, Kogan Page

Clegg, Brian (2000) *Training Plus: Revitalizing your training,* Kogan Page

Forsyth, Patrick (1992) *Running an Effective Training Session,* Gower

Maslow, Abraham (1954) *Motivation and Personality,* Harper

Millbower, Lenn (2000) *Training with a Beat: The teaching power of music,* Kogan Page

Pettigrew, Andrew (1984) *Guide to Trainer Effectiveness,* MSC/ITD

Pfeiffer, J W and Jones, J E (eds) (1994) *The 1974 Handbook for Group Facilitators,* University Associates

Race, Phil (2000) *500 Tips on Group Learning,* Kogan Page

Rae, Leslie (2000) *Effective Planning in Training and Development,* Kogan Page

Rae, Leslie (1999) *Using Evaluation in Training and Development,* Kogan Page

Rae, Leslie (1998a) *Using People Skills in Training and Development,* Kogan Page

Rae, Leslie (1998b) *Using Training Aids in Training and Development,* Kogan Page

Rae, Leslie (1997) *Using Presentations in Training and Development,* Kogan Page

Rae, Leslie (1995) *Techniques of Training,* 3rd edn, Gower

Rae, Leslie (1992) *Guide to In-company Training Methods,* Gower

Siddons, Suzy (1997) *Delivering Training,* CIPD

Spinks, Tony and Clements, Phil (1993) *A Practical Guide to Facilitation Skills,* Kogan Page

Thorne, Kaye and Mackey, David (2000) *Everything You Ever Needed to Know about Training,* 2nd edn, Kogan Page

Tilling, Mike (1999a) *The Induction Organiser,* Gower

Tilling, Mike (1999b) *The Learning Organiser,* Gower

Townsend, John (1996) *The Trainer's Pocketbook,* 8th edn, Management Pocketbooks

Truelove, Steve (1997) *Training in Practice,* Blackwell

Learning

Cotton, Julie (1995a) *The Theory of Learners: An introduction,* Kogan Page

Cotton, Julie (1995b) *The Theory of Learning: An introduction,* Kogan Page

Cotton, Julie (1995c) *The Theory of Learning Strategies: An introduction,* Kogan Page

Honey, Peter and Mumford, Alan (2000a) *Learning Log,* Peter Honey Publications

Honey, Peter and Mumford, Alan (2000b) *The Learning Styles Helper's Guide,* Peter Honey Publications

Honey, Peter and Mumford, Alan (2000c) *The Learning Styles Questionnaire – 80 item version,* Peter Honey Publications

Kolb, David (1984) *Experiential Learning,* Prentice-Hall

Index

CBT (computer-based training)
145–52
CIPD (Chartered Institute of
Personnel and Development)
4
coaching 131–34
communication 153–57
coping with people 166–78
handling difficult people 167–70
handling difficult replies to
questions 166–67
handling difficult situations
170–78

*Glossary of UK Training and
Occupational Learning Terms, A*
(ITOL) vii

Honey, Peter 32

in-company training 130–52
coaching 131–34
computer-based training 145–52
mentoring 134–35
one-to-one instruction 135–39
team development 139–43
induction 2–8
action planning 6–7

GAFO ('Go Away and Find
Out') 2
guidelines 3–7
input sessions 32–47, 48–63
control of time 39–40
during the session 54–62
looking 54–55
making your case 56–57
non-verbal communication
58–60
questioning 60–62
standing/sitting 55–56
using your voice 57–58
environment 44–45
opening 48–53
expectation chart 53
planning and preparation 33–35,
40–43
existing sessions 33–34
new sessions 34–35
presentation skills 35–39,
48–53
butterflies 39
prior to the event 45–46
session plan 42–44
toolkit 46–47

Johari Window 159–62

Kolb, Andrew 32

learning 6–12, 32, 164–65
  competence ladder 164–65
learning cycle 32
Learning Log 8–12

Maslow's hierarchy of needs
  157–59
  viewpoints 157–58
Mehrabian, Professor Albert 58–60
mentoring 6, 134–35
Mumford, Alan 32

Neuro-linguistic Planning (NLP)
  162–64

Pettigrew, Andrew 29–31
  trainer orientation framework
    29–31
Pfeiffer, J W and Jones, J E 28
  T–C training inventory 28

role of the trainer 13–31
  trainer functions 13–17
  trainer knowledge and skills
    17–24
  trainer types 24–31

selecting training strategies 126–29
self-training 130–31, 143–52
  computer-based training
    145–52
  GAFO ('Go Away and Find Out')
    131
  open learning 143–45
speaker impact 58–60

TDNVQ (Training and
    Development National
    Vocational Qualification) 4
Townsend, John 25–27

model of trainer types 25–27
training activities 95–108
  buzz groups 96–97
  demonstrations 101–02
  discussions 98–101
  question and answer 102–04
  short group activities 104–08
    energizers 108
    icebreakers 107–08
    introductory 106–07
  syndicates 97–98
training aids 64–80, 81–94
  audio 89–90
  computer 91–94
  flipchart 66–72
    presentation tips 67–72
  handouts 81–89
    writing 85–89
  object 65
  overhead projector 74–79
    keystoning 76–79
  presenter 65–66
  videos 90–91
  whiteboard 72–73
training approaches 32–47, 48–63,
    109–29, 130–52
  action learning 125–26
    support groups 126
  action mazes 122
  brainstorming 122–23
  case studies 116–18
  computers 91–94, 123–25,
    145–52
  group activities 109–14
  in-company training 130–52
  input sessions 32–47, 48–63
  in-tray/basket 119–22
  role playing 114–16
  selecting appropriate strategy
    126–29
  simulations 119–121

training definitions   vii–viii
training functions   13–17
  e-trainer   16–17
  facilitator   14
  internal consultant-adviser   15

trainer/tutor   14
trainer of trainers   15–16
training designer   16
workplace instructor   13–14